Friendly
Macintosh

Friendly Computer Books are available for the following major software programs:

Friendly DOS 6
by The LeBlond Group

Friendly Access
by Douglas Hergert

Friendly Macintosh
by Kay Yarborough Nelson

Friendly PCs
by Mary Campbell

Friendly Excel 4.0 for Windows
by Jack Nimersheim

Friendly Quicken for Windows
by The LeBlond Group

Friendly Windows 3.1
by Kay Yarborough Nelson

Friendly Word for Windows
by Jack Nimersheim

Friendly WordPerfect
by Kay Yarborough Nelson

Friendly Macintosh

Kay Yarborough Nelson

RANDOM HOUSE
ELECTRONIC PUBLISHING

Friendly Macintosh

Copyright © 1993 by Kay Yarborough Nelson

Produced by MicroText Productions
Composed by Context Publishing Services

Published in the United States by Random House, Inc., New York, and simultaneously in Canada by Random House of Canada, Limited.

Manufactured in Canada.

0 9 8 7 6 5 4 3 2 1

First edition

ISBN 0-679-79191-4

New York   Toronto   London   Sydney   Auckland

Contents

16 **Using the Filing System**   85

17 **Switching Between Programs**   91

18 **The Performa**   93

19 **At Ease**   103

20 **The Desk Accessories**   111

26 Important Information   153

27 Getting Out of Trouble   163

Epilogue: Where to Go from Here   169

Index   173

Preface

Most of us become computer users because we have to, because knowledge of a particular software package is needed for a job, or because computer-assisted productivity is essential to success in business. There are hundreds of reasons. Computers and software are only the means to an end. They have become a necessity of life, and this requirement shapes the way we go about learning how to use software.

Not everyone is interested in every detail of a particular program. Here is a quick, no-nonsense introduction that teaches the basic skills needed to use the software.

In approximately 200 pages, each Friendly Computer Book covers the basic features of a specific popular software in a way that will get new users up and running quickly. The result is a series of computer books that has these unifying characteristics:

- **Topic-oriented organization.** Short, self-contained lessons focus on a particular topic or area that is important in learning to use the software. When you finish the lesson, you'll have mastered an aspect of the software.

- **Spacious layout.** Large type and a spacious layout make the books easy on the eyes and easy to use.
- **Step-by-step approach.** Numbered lists help you to concentrate on the practical steps needed to get your work done.
- **Numerous screen shots.** Each lesson contains at least two screen shots that show you exactly how your screen should look.
- **Frequent use of icons.** Many eye-catching icons—drawing attention to important aspects of the text and software—are placed throughout the book.
- **Lay-flat binding.** Friendly Computer Books stay open as you work.
- **And finally, a low, low price.**

For many users Friendly Computer Books are all they'll need. For others who want to learn more about the software, we've suggested further readings.

Enjoy the friendly approach of Friendly Computer Books!

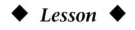

◆ Lesson ◆

1

Getting Started

Once you've unpacked your Macintosh and hooked it up, the first step in getting started is to switch it on. Depending on which model you have, the power switch is in different places.

- If you have one of the compact Macs such as the Classic (Figure 1.1), the power switch is on the back of the computer. That switch turns on both the computer and the screen, because the screen's built in.
- If you have an LC, the power switch is at the back, and you have to turn on the power to the screen by pressing the button on the front of the monitor, near the bottom.
- If you have a larger, modular Macintosh (Figure 1.2), one that has a separate screen, the power switch is probably on the keyboard. It's a large key at the top, and it has a triangle on it. This key turns on both the computer and the screen. On non-Apple keyboards, there may be a round button at the top of the keyboard.

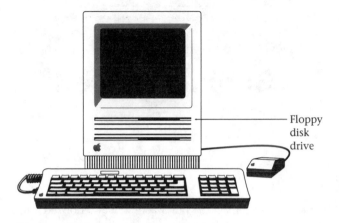

Floppy
disk
drive

Figure 1.1   A compact Macintosh

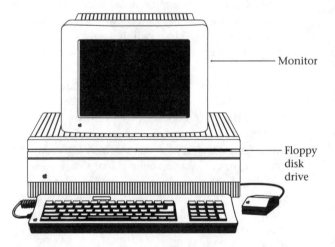

Monitor

Floppy
disk
drive

Figure 1.2   A modular Macintosh

- If you have a PowerBook, press the button on the back to turn it on. If it's "sleeping," you can just press any key to activate it.

If you have an external hard disk, switch it on before you turn on your Macintosh. If you've just bought your computer, though, it's unlikely that you'll have an extra hard disk yet. But if you're practicing at someone else's Mac, there may be a square box to the left or right of the computer. That's probably an external hard disk. Ask its owner.

Once You've Started

When your Macintosh comes on, you'll hear a beep or a chime, you should see a small "happy Mac" icon on the screen, and you'll then go to the desktop, as you'll see in the next lesson.

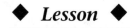

◆ *Lesson* ◆

2

Your Desktop

Now that you've started your Mac, you'll see the desktop on your screen (Figure 2.1). Yours won't look exactly like this one, but it will be similar. If you see a completely different screen, either you're using a special kind of Macintosh called a Performa or a special program called At Ease has been installed on your Mac. Both of these make a Macintosh even easier to use.

- If you see a window called Launcher, you're using a Performa. Turn to Lesson 18 to see more about how to start using a Performa.
- If you see a large file folder, At Ease has been installed on your Macintosh. Lesson 19 shows you more about how At Ease works.

The desktop is also called the Finder, because it's where you find things that have been stored on your computer—programs, documents, graphics, even games. The Finder keeps track of everything. You can call it either the Finder or the desktop; it doesn't matter which.

5

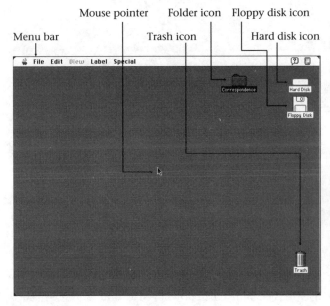

Figure 2.1   The Desktop

On your desktop, tiny icons represent different things. The icon at the upper right corner represents your hard disk. Any floppy disk that you've inserted in your floppy disk drive appears as a tiny floppy disk. The trash can at the bottom of the screen represents the Trash—you use it to get rid of stuff you don't want any more. Depending on who's been using your Macintosh, you also may see tiny folders representing places where documents and programs have been stored, or you may see icons representing programs and documents. Just like on your real desktop, folders can contain other folders with many different things in them, as you'll see later.

Across the top of the screen are the **menus**. Even the two tiny icons at the far right of the menu bar are menus. You'll use menus in all the programs you work with on your Macintosh, but to use a menu, you need to use a mouse, as you'll see in the next lesson.

◆ *Lesson* ◆

3

Working with the Mouse or Trackball

If you haven't used a **mouse** before, it probably will take a little getting used to. If you have a portable Mac like a PowerBook, you have a trackball instead of a mouse. Try the practice exercises in this lesson for the mouse and the trackball.

Tip
At Ease comes with an easy Mouse Practice tutorial with sound and animation. If you have At Ease, you may want to take that tutorial.

Clicking and Double-Clicking with the Mouse

1. Move the mouse on your desktop, and you'll see that the pointer on the screen moves, too.
2. Pick the mouse up and notice that the pointer stays in place on the screen. *It's OK to pick up the mouse.*

Figure 3.1   The Trash window

3. Move the mouse pointer to the Trash and **click** the button on the mouse once. You'll see the Trash change color. When an icon is dark, that means it's **selected**. You have to select something before you can do anything with it.

4. Now try **double-clicking**. Instead of clicking once, click twice, quickly. The Trash window should open (Figure 3.1). Notice that the Trash icon is gray now, indicating that it's been opened.

5. To close the Trash window, move the mouse pointer to the tiny box in the upper left corner of the window and click once.

You click once to select an item or close a window. Clicking twice, or double-clicking, opens an icon to show you what's in it. If the icon represents a program or document, double-clicking on it actually starts the program, as you'll see soon.

Dragging

Dragging is another basic mouse technique. You drag to move icons around on the screen, select several icons at once, or choose commands from menus. To drag, press the mouse button and hold it down while you move the mouse.

1. Try dragging the Trash to a different spot on the desktop. Click once on it, hold the button down, and move the mouse on your real desktop. Watch the screen as the Trash moves, too. Release the mouse button, and the Trash stays where you put it.

2. Drag the Trash back to its original place at the lower right corner of the screen.

3. Try opening a menu and choosing a command. Move the mouse pointer to the tiny apple on the far left of the menu bar. Click once on it, keep the mouse button down, and drag straight down. When About This Computer is highlighted, release the mouse button.

You'll see the **dialog box** in Figure 3.2. It's telling you the version of system software you're using and showing how your computer is using memory. Dialog boxes appear whenever the Macintosh needs to tell you something or to get information from you.

Click once in the tiny box at the upper left of the dialog box to close it. That box, by the way, is called the **close box**.

Tip

Remember, dragging is a three-step process: Click on what you want, keeping the mouse button down; move the mouse; then release the mouse button.

Try dragging to choose items from menus until you feel comfortable with the process. If a command you choose opens a dialog box, just close it by clicking on its close box or Cancel button, if it has one.

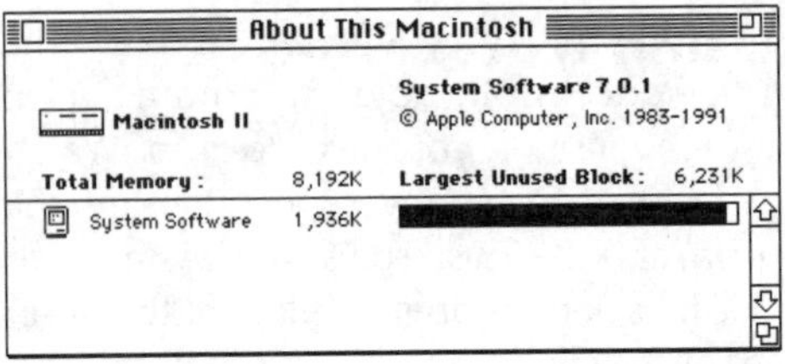

Figure 3.2   Getting information about
your computer

Try This Mouse Trick

If you really can't get used to the mouse, try this trick.
Switch the mouse to your other hand and use it for a
while. If you're right-handed, try it in your left hand.
When you switch back, you'll be amazed at how much
more comfortable it feels.

Left-Handed?

If you're left-handed, you may want to connect the mouse
to the left side of your keyboard. Many keyboards let you
do this. Turn off the power to your computer before you
switch, though.

The Mouse Pad

You may have a mouse pad on your (real) desktop. It's
there to provide traction for the mouse. If you don't have
a mouse pad, the pointer may move in jerks across the
screen. If you don't have one, you can use a sheet of
paper.

Using a Trackball

If you have a PowerBook, you don't have a mouse at all. Instead, you've got a **trackball**. You move the mouse pointer by rolling the trackball with your fingers, and you press a key to click.

1. Try moving the mouse pointer by rolling the trackball.
2. To click, press the button above or below the trackball. You can do this with a finger or a thumb. Many people find that clicking with the thumb is easier.
3. To drag, keep the button down while you roll the trackball. You'll need to train that finger or thumb to stay down on the key while you're dragging.
4. Try choosing About This Macintosh from the Apple menu. Move the mouse pointer to the tiny apple on the far left of the menu bar. Click once on it by pressing the button, keep the button down, and roll the trackball. When About This Macintosh is highlighted, release the button.
5. To close the About This Macintosh dialog box, click once on the tiny close box at the upper left of the window.

Try practicing with the trackball or mouse on your own. You'll get more practice selecting, double-clicking, and dragging in the rest of the lessons, too.

4

Your Keyboard

If you're new to the Macintosh, there probably are some keys that you've never seen before on your keyboard. Look at your own keyboard as you follow along, because there are different Macintosh keyboards. There's a standard keyboard for older Macintosh models as well as a newer one, and there also are "extended" keyboards that have extra function keys on them. You won't need those function keys if you're just starting out.

Starting with the Power On key, if your keyboard has one, we'll go clockwise.

Power On key   The Power On key is a large key with a triangle on it, which turns on some Macintoshes. You may or may not have one, depending on which Macintosh you have.

Delete   Pressing the Delete key lets you delete text you've selected. To delete icons, you drag them to the Trash. If you have a very old keyboard, this key may be labeled Backspace.

15

Return

The Return key, sometimes called the Enter key, works differently, depending on what you're doing with your Macintosh. For example, if you're working in a program, such as a word processing program, you press the Return key to end a paragraph or insert a blank line (by pressing it twice). In dialog boxes, you can press Return instead of clicking on a button that has a thick border around it; many OK buttons work this way. If you press Return after you've selected an icon, you can type a new name for the icon.

Shift

There's a Shift key on the right side of the keyboard as well as on the left. Press the Shift key to type uppercase characters.

Arrow keys

You may have a separate pad of arrow keys, or they may be next to letter keys, depending on the keyboard you're using. The arrow keys can move the highlight in a window or take you up or down a list of items without using the mouse. Most of the time, you'll be using the mouse while you're learning the Mac, but the arrow keys are an alternate to use if your mouse freezes up. Once you become a power user, you'll find that you use the keyboard a lot more than you think you will now.

Numeric keypad

The numeric keypad is on the right side of your keyboard. Use it like a pocket calculator for entering numbers. You can use the Enter key on the numeric keypad as the Return key, too. Press the Clear key (the first one on the numeric keypad) if it isn't producing numbers and you want it to. If it's not producing numbers, you can use the numeric keypad just like the arrow keys.

Space bar

The space bar is the biggest key on your keyboard. You use it, of course, to insert spaces. But unlike on a typewriter, you'll usually insert spaces in your documents by using the Tab key to align text. Also, try not to type two spaces between sentences; the computer takes care of that for you.

⌘

The ⌘ key is just to the left of the space bar. It's the weird one with the tiny apple and the cloverleaf-shaped symbol on it. This is the key you'll use for most keyboard shortcuts, such as ⌘-S for Save. By the way, whenever you see a key combination connected with a hyphen like this, it means "press both of these keys at the same time," so you'd press ⌘ and s at once. You don't have to press the Shift key to get a capital S.

Option   The Option key is to the left of the ⌘ key. It's always used in combination with other keys. One of its main uses is for creating special characters and closing windows in a hurry.

Ctrl   The Ctrl, or control, key is another one that, like the Option key, is used only in combination with other keys. It's not found on all keyboards, so don't search for it if you don't see it right away.

Shift   The Shift key works just as it does on a typewriter. Use it to get uppercase characters.

Caps Lock   When Caps Lock is down, you'll be typing in ALL CAPS until you press the Shift key, which switches you to lowercase. One exception: The symbols above the numbers on the top row aren't produced when Caps Lock is down. Look at the indicator light on your keyboard, if it has one, to see if Caps Lock is on. If it's on, press Caps Lock again to turn it off.

Tab   The Tab key inserts a tab (a fixed amount of space) in a document. You'll use it to indent and line up text in word processing programs. In spreadsheets, the Tab key usually moves you from one cell to another. You also use the Tab key to move through dialog boxes, as you'll see later.

Esc   The Esc, or escape, key is hardly ever used, either. In a dialog box, you can press it to close the box without making any changes. In some programs, you can press it to undo something you just did.

Number keys   The number and symbol keys across the top row are the same as on a typewriter, but you may see a tilde key (~) that's new. On some keyboards, that tilde key is to the left of the space bar.

If you aren't using a standard Apple keyboard or if you're using a PowerBook, the placement of some of these keys may be a little different. I use a DataDesk keyboard, for example, and I have two ⌘ keys as well as separate Paste, Cut, Home, End, Page Up, and Page Down keys.

Although most of the time you'll use the mouse, especially while you're getting used to the Macintosh, using the keyboard does give you some good shortcuts. Keyboard shortcuts for menu commands are listed on the menus. For example, pressing ⌘-S is much faster than choosing Save from a File menu, and pressing ⌘-Y to eject a floppy disk is another quick shortcut. After you've had a chance to use your Mac for a while, Lesson 25 will show you some more shortcuts.

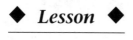

◆ *Lesson* ◆

5

Icons

The tiny graphic images on your screen are **icons**. They represent all sorts of things—programs, folders, disks, documents, and many other things, too (Figure 5.1). Double-clicking on an icon starts the program it represents, or opens a disk or folder icon so you can see what's in it.

When you start your Macintosh, you'll always see the icon of the startup disk in the upper right corner of the screen. You may not have many other icons on your screen if you have a new Macintosh, so let's create some.

1. First, close any windows you may have opened.
2. Select New Folder from the File menu. Move the mouse pointer to the word *File*, press the mouse button, and move the mouse down. When New Folder is highlighted, let go of the mouse button. You'll see an empty folder on your screen (Figure 5.2).
3. To create another empty folder, choose New Folder from the File menu again, or try this keyboard short-

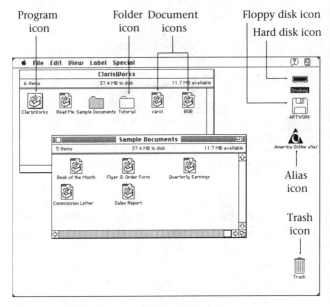

Program icon   Folder Document icons   Floppy disk icon
Hard disk icon

Alias icon

Trash icon

Figure 5.1   Different kinds of icons

cut: Press the ⌘ key and the **n** key at the same time. You'll see another empty folder, this one labeled "empty folder 2" with a box around its name (Figure 5.3).

Figure 5.2
Creating
an empty folder

You can just start typing to give the folder a better name. After you press Return or click somewhere else with the mouse, your new folder will jump to its proper alphabetical place in the list. In a long list, it sometimes disappears from the screen! Just type the first letter of its name, and you should see it again.

Figure 5.3   Creating another empty folder

   Tip

It's easy to overlook that there's a box around an icon's name and to just start typing one thing when you think you're typing something else. You can rename an icon by mistake this way. So can your cat, if it walks across the keyboard. If this happens *and the box is still around the icon's name*, just choose Undo from the Edit menu or press ⌘-Z.

Renaming Icons

"Empty folder" and "empty folder 2" don't say much, although it's true that there's nothing in these folders yet. Let's try renaming them.

1. Type a new name for empty folder 2, such as **My Folder**. Since the box is already around the icon's name, just start typing.

2. To rename the other empty folder, click on its name to select it and produce the box. If you click on the icon part instead of the name, sometimes you won't see the box. If that happens, click again on the name so that the box appears.

3. Type a new name, such as **My Other Folder**, and press the Return key, or click somewhere else.

If you make a mistake, press the Delete key to erase it.

Tip

To rename an icon, click on its name. When you see the box, type a new name. Moving the mouse slightly after you click makes the box appear faster. You can rename any icon this way. It's not a good idea to rename icons that represent programs, though. And don't rename your System Folder or anything that's in it.

Moving Icons

You've already seen that you can drag an icon to move it. You can move icons into different folders or out of folders and onto the desktop.

1. Click on My Folder and drag it to My Other Folder. When My Other Folder turns dark, release the mouse button. Now all you see is My Other Folder, because My Folder's inside it.
2. Double-click on My Other Folder, and you'll see My Folder in an open window (Figure 5.4). My Other Folder's icon is gray, which means that it's been opened.
3. Drag My Folder out of the open window onto the desktop.
4. Now drag My Folder back into the open window. You can drag icons to other icons, such as floppy disk icons, to open windows, and to the desktop.

Opened icon   Open window

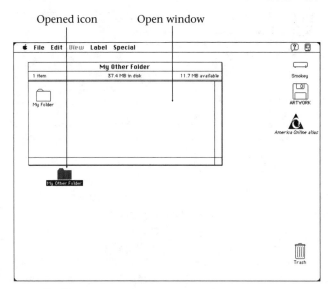

Figure 5.4 Opened icons are gray

  Tip
If you drag a document icon onto a program icon
and the program icon turns dark, the program will
open the document if you release the mouse button.

Opening a Disk Icon

To see what's on a disk, double-click on its icon, just as
you do to open a folder.

Name	Size	Kind	Label	Last Modified
▷ ☐ Aldus PageMaker 4.0	–	folder	–	Tue, Jan 12, 1993, 2:34 PM
▷ ☐ AOL	–	folder	–	Wed, Jun 17, 1992, 1:20 PM
▷ ☐ Apple File Exchange Folder	–	folder	–	Sat, Jun 13, 1992, 8:08 AM
☐ ART	50K	PageMaker 4.0 doc...	–	Mon, Sep 28, 1992, 1:35 PM
▷ ☐ BBS folder icons	–	folder	–	Thu, Apr 8, 1993, 3:21 PM
☐ *Capture alias*	1K	alias	–	Mon, Oct 12, 1992, 9:16 AM
▷ ☐ Capture Utilities	–	folder	–	Tue, Sep 25, 1990, 9:02 AM
▷ ☐ ClarisWorks	–	folder	–	Fri, Apr 9, 1993, 9:23 AM
▷ ☐ Disk Utilities	–	folder	Hot	Fri, Apr 9, 1993, 9:20 AM
☒ FastCopy	116K	application program	–	Mon, Sep 24, 1990, 4:31 PM
☒ Font Downloader	79K	application program	Hot	Mon, Jan 21, 1991, 8:41 AM

Figure 5.5   The contents of my hard disk

Double-click on the icon of your hard disk (mine is
named Smokey) to see what's been stored on it. A window
will open, showing its contents (Figure 5.5).

Practice dragging icons to the desktop or in and out of
folders until you feel comfortable with moving icons
around. If you forget which folder an icon originally came
from, just click on it to select it and then press ⌘-Y or
choose Put Away from the File menu, and it'll go back
where it belongs.

Don't move any icons out of your System Folder.
Your Macintosh needs those icons left there.

The Trash

Now you'll get to see how the Trash really works. To delete something from your desktop, you drag it to the Trash.

Let's delete one of the folders you created in the preceding lesson, since there's nothing in them anyway.

• Drag My Folder to the Trash and release the mouse button when the Trash icon turns dark. If you don't release the button when the Trash is highlighted, the folder icon just sits near or on top of the Trash. Release the button when the Trash is dark, and the folder disappears. Notice that the Trash can bulges when it has something in it (Figure 6.1).

Trash

Figure 6.1
The Trash bulges when it has something in it.

The folder's in the Trash, but it hasn't been deleted yet, because your Macintosh won't delete anything until you tell it to by choosing Empty Trash from the Special menu.

• Choose Empty Trash from the Special menu.

Figure 6.2   Click OK to delete what's in the Trash.

You'll see a dialog box asking you to be sure that you really want to delete what's in it (Figure 6.2).

Tip

If you want to bypass this dialog box, press the Option key while you drag the icon to the Trash.

• Click OK to delete My Folder.

If you ever need to get something back before you've emptied the Trash, you can double-click on the Trash icon to open it and see what's in it. Then drag what you want to keep out of the Trash window and put it in a folder on the desktop.

Tip

Dragging a floppy disk icon to the Trash is a neat shortcut for ejecting the disk from your floppy drive. It doesn't erase the disk or delete anything that's on it, as you might expect.

◆ *Lesson* ◆

7

Working with Disks

You use 3.5-inch disks with your Macintosh. They're encased in plastic, so they're not too fragile, but you should still be careful with them.

- Don't try to open the metal shutter to see what's inside the plastic case.
- Keep disks away from magnets, which can erase everything on a disk. There are magnets in stereo speakers and telephones. There may be a magnetic paper clip holder on your desk.

Disk Capacities

There are two kinds of floppy disks, and they look almost exactly alike (Figure 7.1). Double-density disks hold about 800K (kilobytes) of data, and high-density disks hold 1.4Mb (megabytes). That's a lot of information. For example, you can write a book over twice as long as this one and store it all on one 800K disk.

Figure 7.1   A floppy disk

Here's how to tell them apart: High-density disks usually are labeled "HD" and they always have two square holes. Double-density disks have only one square hole.

Some older Macintoshes can accept only double-density disks, but most that are made nowadays can accept both types of disk.

> **Tip**
> If you have a Performa, buy at least two boxes of high-density disks (20 disks). You'll need them to back up the programs that came installed on your Performa. Better get an extra box of floppies for storing your work on, too.

Formatting Disks

When you buy disks, they're usually not formatted, although you can buy preformatted disks at a premium price. Before you can use a new floppy disk, you'll probably need to initialize it. When you put a new disk in your

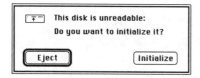

Figure 7.2 Initializing a disk

floppy drive, your Macintosh will tell you the disk needs to be initialized (Figure 7.2). If you're using a double-density disk, you'll be asked whether you want One-Sided or Two-Sided. Click Two-Sided; one-sided disks are hardly ever used any more.

If you're sure it's a brand-new disk, go ahead and click Initialize. If it's a disk that's already been used, it may have information on it, and initializing will erase that information. Be sure there's nothing you want on a disk before you initialize it.

1. Insert a new floppy disk into the drive. Insert the disk with the label side facing up and the metal shutter going into the slot first. The round metal button side should be *down*, or facing *away* from you if your Macintosh sits on its side.
2. When the Macintosh asks you whether to initialize the disk, click Initialize.

After the disk is initialized, you'll be asked to give it a name. Use one that helps you keep track of what you're planning to store on the disk.

Tip
Don't leave all your disks named "Untitled."

Ejecting Disks

Once you put a disk in your floppy drive, how do you get it out again? Easy. Click on its icon to select it. Then drag the disk icon to the Trash, and it will pop out of the disk drive. Pull it the rest of the way out.

- Eject the disk you just initialized.

Tip
You also can click on the disk icon to select it, and press ⌘-Y or choose Put Away from the File menu to eject it.

Copying Disks

It's often convenient to make a copy of an entire floppy disk all at once. If you have two floppy disk drives, all you have to do is put one disk into each drive and drag the icon of the disk that you're copying onto the icon of the disk that's going to be the copy.

With only one floppy drive, however, copying disks is a little different:

1. Put the disk you want to copy in the floppy drive. Then choose Eject Disk from the Special menu. Be sure to use this command to eject the disk; don't drag its icon to the Trash. A dimmed image of the disk remains on the desktop.

2. Put the disk that you want to be the copy in the floppy drive.

Figure 7.3
Drag one disk icon over the other to copy.

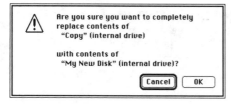

Figure 7.4   Copying a disk

> This can be a new disk or a disk that you want to reuse.
>
> **3.** Drag the icon of the dimmed floppy disk (the first one) over the icon of the disk you just put in—the one you want to be the copy (Figure 7.3). You'll see a warning dialog box (Figure 7.4). Click OK to continue.

You'll be asked to insert disks as needed as the copy is made. To stop the copy process if you change your mind, press ⌘-.

Tip

To lock a disk so that what's on it can't be changed, open its write-protect slot. It's a good idea to lock program disks after you copy their contents onto your hard disk. You'll see how to copy like this in the next lesson.

Erasing Disks

To recycle a used disk, erasing everything that's on it, select its icon on the desktop. Then choose Erase Disk from the Special menu. You'll be asked to make sure you really want to do this, because erasing, like initializing, removes all data from the disk.

 Never try to erase your hard disk.

◆ *Lesson* ◆

8

Copying Documents and Programs

As you work with your Macintosh, you'll often find that you want to copy documents onto floppy disks so that you can give them to someone else or make backup copies for safekeeping. When you buy new programs, you put them on your Macintosh by copying their icons onto your hard disk icon. And sometimes you'll want to make an extra copy of something on the same disk. There are different ways to copy, depending on what you want to copy.

Copying Icons on the Same Disk

You'll frequently need to make a copy, or duplicate, of a document. The Macintosh has a built-in command for this.

1. Select the icon you want to copy by clicking on it once. Select My Other Folder, for example.
2. Choose Duplicate from the File menu (or press ⌘-D).

Figure 8.1   Duplicating an icon

You'll get a copy of the icon—an exact duplicate of what it represents (Figure 8.1). If you duplicate a folder, all the items in it are copied.

Notice that the copy is named the same as the original, with "copy" added. There's a box around the name, so you can rename the copy as soon as it's created if you want to.

> ### Tip
> If you can drag an icon from one folder to another on the same disk, it will just be moved, not copied. Press the Option key while you drag to make a copy on the same disk. Or use the Duplicate command (⌘-D) and then drag the copy where you want it.

Copying Documents

Instead of copying entire folders, you'll often want to copy just a few file icons from one folder to another or to a different disk. Now that you know how to copy, you can put a few practice icons in a folder.

1. Double-click on your hard disk's icon and duplicate three or four file icons, just for practice.
2. Drag your practice icons to My Other Folder.

Figure 8.2 Selecting icons by dragging

3. Double-click on My Other Folder to open it if it's not already open.

4. Instead of dragging icons one by one, you can select several of them at once. Click just outside the group of icons; then drag the selection rectangle over them to select them (Figure 8.2). Once they're selected, you can drag the whole selection at once. This works well if the icons are next to each other.

5. If the icons aren't next to each other, use the Shift-click technique. Press the Shift key, keep it down, and click on each icon you want to select. You'll see each icon become highlighted as you click on it (Figure 8.3). When you've selected all the icons you want, you can drag them all at the same time.

Tip

If you select an icon and decide you *don't* want it selected, just click anywhere outside it to deselect it.

Practice using the two different selection techniques on the icons in My Other Folder. Remember, they're dupli-

Figure 8.3   Selecting icons by Shift-clicking

cates, so you can drag them to the Trash when you're done.

Copying to and from Floppy Disks

You'll often need to copy documents from your hard disk to your floppy disks so that you can give them to other people, take them to another computer, or simply keep a safe backup copy away from your hard disk for long-term storage. To copy a document onto a floppy disk from your hard disk, just drag its icon to the floppy disk's icon. When the floppy disk's icon turns dark, release the mouse button. Try this if you have a floppy disk handy.

> **Tip**
> Be sure to put a paper label on your floppy disks and write on the label what you copied so that you can easily locate what's on those disks later.

You'll need to copy items from floppy disks onto your hard disk, too. To do this, double-click on the floppy disk

icon and drag the icons of the items you want copied onto
your hard disk icon.

Tip

Be sure to drag the icons to the *hard disk icon* or to
a *folder icon* on your hard disk. If you simply drag
them to the desktop, they aren't copied or moved,
and they'll disappear when you eject the floppy
disk.

Copying Programs

If a program doesn't come with its own Installer, you
usually can just drag a program's icon from the floppy
disk onto your hard disk's icon to install it. Open the
floppy disk icon first by double-clicking on it, then drag
the program and any files it needs to a folder on your hard
disk. You can't drag a floppy disk icon to your hard disk
icon to copy everything on it.

Tip

It's a good idea to organize your hard disk into
folders, instead of keeping absolutely everything
"loose" on your hard disk. Create a folder for a
program *before* you copy it.

Ready to take a break? If you're not using a PowerBook,
to turn off your Macintosh, choose Shut Down from the
Special menu (Figure 8.4). Then turn off the power to your
computer and monitor, too, if you have a separate monitor. On the bigger Macs, choosing Shut Down turns off

Figure 8.4   Choose Shut Down
before you turn off your Macintosh.

the power for you. Your PowerBook will go to sleep if
you're just taking a short break.

Always be sure to choose Shut Down before you turn off
the power, or you may lose some of your work.

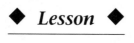

◆ *Lesson* ◆

9

Windows

As you've been working along with these lessons, you've been opening and closing windows. Now it's time to take a closer look at how they work.

As you've seen, if you double-click on a folder icon, it opens a window to show what's in the folder. If you double-click on a disk icon, a window opens to show you what's on the disk. Figure 9.1 illustrates the different parts of a window.

- Double-click on your hard disk icon to open a window so you can follow along in this lesson.

You know by now that you use the **close box** to close the window, but there are other built-in controls in a window.

The Title Bar

The **title bar** shows the window's title. If the title bar isn't showing gray lines, the window isn't active. Only one window can be active at a time. To make a window active, just click on it.

Close box   Header   Title bar   Zoom box

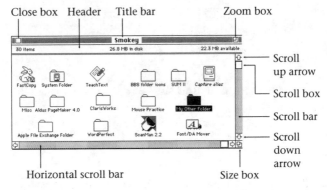

Horizontal scroll bar   Size box

Figure 9.1   Parts of a window

   Tip
You can drag a window by its title bar to move it.

The Zoom Box

The **Zoom box** is a neat built-in control that enlarges the window or makes it the original size again.

1. Click on the Zoom box to enlarge your window.
2. Click it again to return the window to the size it was before.

The Scroll Bars

If a window's scroll bars are gray, there's more to see than what the window's displaying.

- To scroll through the contents of your window, click on the **scroll arrow** at the bottom of the scroll bar.

Keep the mouse button down and watch the window's contents move.

Tip

Click in the middle of the scroll bar to go to the middle of the window, or click at the top or bottom to go to the beginning or end of what's in the window.

If the horizontal scroll bar at the bottom of the window is gray, there's more to see to the right or left. You can click the scroll arrow in this scroll bar to scroll horizontally.

The Header

The **header** shows information about what's in that particular window, such as how many items are in that folder or how much space is left on a disk.

The Size Box

You'll frequently need to make a window larger or smaller, and the built-in **size box** lets you do just that.

- Click in the window's size box and drag the borders inward or outward to change the window's size.

Try practicing with your window—opening and closing it, moving it by dragging its title bar, resizing it with the Size box, and enlarging it with the Zoom box until you feel comfortable with these techniques.

◆ *Lesson* ◆

10

More About Windows

You don't have to always look at icons in a window. In fact, there are quite a few different ways to look at the contents of a window. To change views, you use the View menu (Figure 10.1).

• Choose by Name from the View menu. You'll see the contents of the window listed by name (Figure 10.2). After you have a lot of files and folders on your Macintosh, you may want to view them by name most of the time, because a list takes up lots less space than icons. But at first, it's a lot more fun to look at all the icons.

Figure 10.1 The View menu

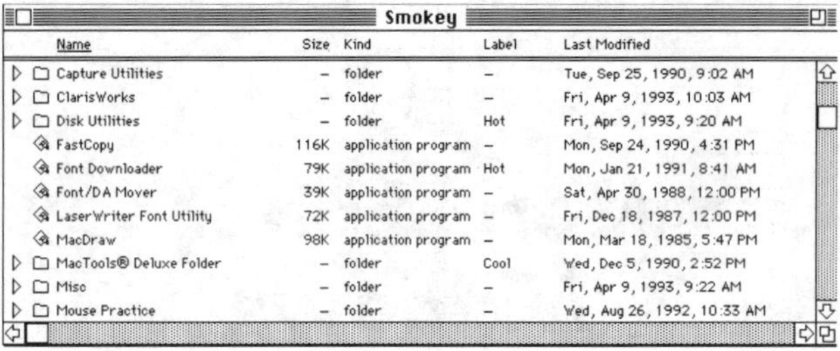

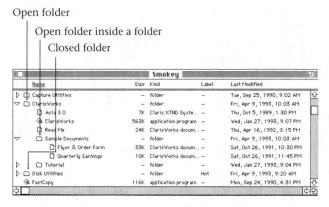

Figure 10.2 Viewing a window by name

When you view by Name, a folder that's closed has a right-pointing arrow to the left of its name. An open folder has a down-pointing arrow next to its name (Figure 10.3).

1. Click on an arrow to see what's in a closed folder.
2. To close the folder, click on the arrow again.

Open folder

   Open folder inside a folder

      Closed folder

Figure 10.3 Open and closed folders

Name	Size	Kind	Label	Last Modified
▷ ☐ Capture Utilities	–	folder	–	Tue, Sep 25, 1990, 9:02 AM
▷ ☐ ClarisWorks	–	folder	–	Fri, Apr 9, 1993, 10:03 AM
▷ ☐ Disk Utilities	–	folder	Hot	Fri, Apr 9, 1993, 9:20 AM
◈ FastCopy	116K	application program	–	Mon, Sep 24, 1990, 4:31 PM
◈ Font Downloader	79K	application program	Hot	Mon, Jan 21, 1991, 8:41 AM
◈ Font/DA Mover	39K	application program	–	Sat, Apr 30, 1988, 12:00 PM
◈ LaserWriter Font Utility	72K	application program	–	Fri, Dec 18, 1987, 12:00 PM
◈ MacDraw	98K	application program	–	Mon, Mar 18, 1985, 5:47 PM
▷ ☐ MacTools® Deluxe Folder	–	folder	Cool	Wed, Dec 5, 1990, 2:52 PM
▷ ☐ Misc	–	folder	–	Fri, Apr 9, 1993, 9:22 AM
▷ ☐ Mouse Practice	–	folder	–	Wed, Aug 26, 1992, 10:33 AM

Figure 10.4   Select items by dragging

You also can select items when you're viewing by name,
just as you can when you're viewing by icon. To select
items that are next to each other, click next to the first
one and then drag the selection rectangle that you'll see,
until the last item you want to select is highlighted (Figure 10.4).

- To deselect the group, just click anywhere outside it.
- To select items that aren't next to each other, Shift-
  click on them, just as you did in Lesson 8. To deselect
  just one item, click on it again.

Tip

To sort the list that's showing in a window, click
on one of the headings at the top. For example, to
first see files listed with the ones you worked on
most recently, click Last Modified. To sort them
alphabetically by name, click Name.

There are other views, but by Icon or by Name are the
ones you'll use most. You can try the other views by

choosing them from the View menu. Try by Small Icon and you will see that you can fit more icons in a window.

Tip
Windows in the Finder show special **outline views** when you're viewing by anything other than Icon or Small icon. This makes it easier to see where you are in your filing system.

Now let's look at a few more techniques you can use with windows. Try these out as you read about them.

Closing All the Open Windows

If you open a lot of windows on your desktop, you may be looking at a cluttered desktop very quickly. There's a built-in shortcut for closing all the open windows: Press the Option key and click in the close box of one of the windows, and all of them will close. Remember this trick; it's a good one.

Moving a Window Without Making It Active

You've already seen that you can move a window just by dragging it by its title bar. But every time you click in a window's title bar, it becomes active and appears on top of the stack of windows you were looking at. Sometimes this can drive you crazy, because you don't want to see into that window; you just want to move it out of the

way. To move a window without making it active, press
the ⌘ key and drag it by its title bar.

Selecting Everything in a Window

Instead of dragging or Shift-clicking to select everything
in a window, you can use a handy Select All command on
the Edit menu that will select everything in the window at
once. Pressing ⌘-A is the shortcut. Sometimes it's a lot
faster to select everything and then just Shift-click on a
few items to deselect them if you're selecting most of
what's in a window.

Tip
To close all the open folders in a window, select
them all (with ⌘-A) and then press ⌘-left arrow.

Closing Folders as
You Open New Ones

If you're hunting for a file that's buried several folders
deep, you also can create a lot of clutter on your desktop
by opening window after window. Keep the Option key
down as you open folders, and the folders that are already
open will close as you open new ones.

Looking at the Folders
Your Folder Is In

Sometimes you can get lost in the folder system, especially
if you're looking at a folder that's in a folder that's in a

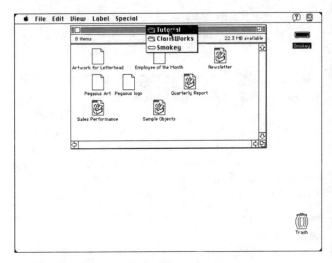

Figure 10.5   Seeing where you are in the folder structure

folder. To see the list of folders leading back to the main folder (which usually is your hard disk), press the ⌘ key and click on the title of the window. You'll see all the folder names leading back up the folder list (Figure 10.5). Be sure to click on the window title, not just somewhere in the title bar.

You're well on your way to becoming a power user! Take a break now, or continue to the next lesson.

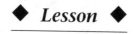

◆ *Lesson* ◆

11

Dialog Boxes

A special kind of window called a **dialog box** appears whenever your Macintosh needs more information from you, or needs to tell you something.

 Tip
Any time you see three dots (..., which are called an **ellipsis**) next to a command's name, or in some programs, an arrow pointing to the right, a dialog box will come up if you choose that command.

Figure 11.1 shows a typical dialog box. Notice that the Yes command has a heavy border around it. You can either click that button with the mouse or just press the Return key to choose Yes.

Dialog boxes sometimes ask you to type information, but sometimes they give you a list of things to choose from, too. And there are built-in tricks in some dialog boxes.

Figure 11.1   A dialog box

- Choose Page Setup from the Find menu, or look at the dialog box in Figure 11.2.

The dialog box you'll see depends on the printer you're using. This particular dialog box belongs to a LaserWriter. If you haven't selected a printer yet, you'll see how to designate one in a later lesson.

The round buttons are called **radio buttons**, and you can choose only one of them at a time. The square boxes are called **check boxes**, and you usually can select more than one of these. If you see a down-pointing arrow or a box with a shadowed border around it like Tabloid in Figure 11.2, clicking on it will display a **pop-up list** that you can make more choices from.

1. Click in the Tabloid box and hold the mouse button down to see the list appear.
2. Click Cancel to close the dialog box.

If a dialog box has a title bar like the one in Figure 11.3, you can move it just like any other window by dragging it by its title bar.

After you've made your selections from a dialog box, click on its OK, Yes, or Start button, or the button that's heavily outlined. If you decide you don't want to make those choices, click its Cancel button. You also can close a dialog box without making any changes by pressing Esc or typing ⌘-. (Command and the period key).

Radio button   Check box

Popup list indicator

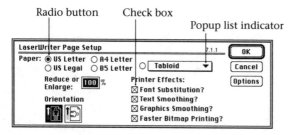

Figure 11.2 The Page Setup dialog box

The dialog boxes you'll most often use in programs are the Open and Save (or Save As). They're for opening and saving the documents you create. These dialog boxes are very similar in any program you use on your Macintosh, so we'll take a closer look at them in Lessons 15 and 16.

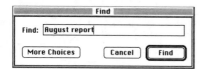

Figure 11.3 A movable dialog box

♦ *Lesson* ♦

12

The Menu System

By now, you're probably wondering what all the commands on those menus are for. In this chapter, we'll take a whirlwind tour through them. Don't worry about learning in detail what each command does! Most of the time you'll use only a very few of the many commands that are on your Macintosh's menus, such as New, Copy, Cut, Paste, and Shut Down. And you may be surprised to find out how many commands you already know about.

We'll start at the far left of the menu bar.

Tip

The menus you see when you use application programs will be a little different, because they'll show the commands that the particular program uses. All programs will have Apple, File, and Edit menus, though.

55

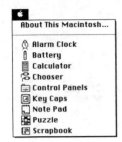

Figure 12.1   The Apple menu

The Apple Menu

- Click on the tiny apple and keep the mouse button down to display the Apple menu.

The Apple menu (Figure 12.1) shows the **desk accessories**, such as the Calculator and Note Pad, that have been installed on your Macintosh. It also gives you access to **control panels** that you use to customize how your Mac works. Lesson 20 shows you more about the desk accessories, and Lesson 21 demonstrates using the control panels.

The Apple menu is very useful, because what's listed on it is also available to you anytime you're using a program. You can put items on the Apple menu yourself; you'll see how later.

The File Menu

- Drag over to the word *File* on the menu bar, or click on File and keep the mouse button down.

The File menu (Figure 12.2) lists the commands that let you manage documents. As you may have figured out by

Figure 12.2 The File menu

now, documents are also called *files*, even if they're budgets, letters to your aunt, or graphic images. All programs have a File menu, and most of the commands on File menus are all the same.

You've already seen how to use several commands on this menu, such as New Folder to create and name a new folder on your desktop, and Duplicate to copy an icon.

The Edit Menu

- Click on Edit on the title bar and keep the mouse button down, or drag over to the word *Edit* to see what's on the Edit menu.

The Edit menu (Figure 12.3) contains commands you'll use often, such as Cut, Copy, and Paste. You'll also use it to see what's on the Clipboard, which is where everything you copy and cut goes. There's an Edit menu in all programs, too. These commands are so important that you'll get a chance to practice them later.

Figure 12.3   The Edit menu has all
the Copy, Cut, and Paste commands.

Tip

If a command on a menu is grayed, that means it
can't be used at this time. For example, you can't
copy something unless you've selected it first.

The View Menu

- Click on View or drag over to it to review the View
  menu's commands.

You've already seen the View menu (Figure 12.4) in
Lesson 10. It lets you choose how you'd like to view items
on your desktop.

Figure 12.4   The View menu

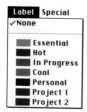

Figure 12.5 The Label menu

The Label Menu

- Click on Label on the menu bar, or drag to it.

The Label menu (Figure 12.5) shows colors and labels that you can assign to your documents and folders to categorize them. For example, you might want to label a spreadsheet budget and a letter as belonging to a project you've started. You can use the Find command to search for all the documents that have the same label, even though they're stored in completely different folders.

You use the Labels control panel to set up your personal system of label names and colors.

The Special Menu

- Click on Special on the menu bar, or drag over to it.

The Special menu (Figure 12.6) is a collection of different commands that let you eject floppy disks, clean up windows, and shut down your Macintosh.

Figure 12.6   The Special menu

The one thing to remember about the Special menu is this: *Always use it to shut down your Macintosh.*

The Help Menu

That tiny question mark is a menu, too. It's the Help menu.

- Click on the question mark icon at the right side of the screen, and drag to select Show Balloons.

The Help menu (Figure 12.7) lets you get help for what you're doing as you work. After you've selected Show Balloons, as you move the mouse pointer around on the screen, a little balloon appears with a message about what the item you're pointing at does (Figure 12.8).

- Move the mouse pointer to various icons on your screen, and read the balloon help about them.

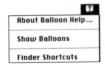

Figure 12.7   The Help menu

Figure 12.8 Getting Balloon help

Anytime you need to figure out what a strange-looking icon does, turn on balloon help and check it out. These balloons get in your way most of the time, though.

- To turn off Balloon help, select it from the Help menu again.

The Application Menu

The tiny icon at the far right of the menu bar is the Application menu. It indicates which program or desk accessory is active.

- Click on the Application menu icon to display the Application menu (Figure 12.9).

A check mark next to a program's name indicates that it's active. You can have several programs running at once

Figure 12.9 The Application Menu

and switch among them by selecting the one you want from this Application menu, as you'll see in a later lesson.

Right now, the only program you're using is the Finder, so a small Finder icon appears there. After you become familiar with the icons that represent programs and desk accessories, you'll be able to tell which one is active by glancing at the tiny icon on the menu bar.

Ready for a break? Or continue on as we explore a few more desktop tricks in the next lesson.

13

Working with Your Desktop

As you work with your Macintosh, your desktop may get cluttered. In this lesson you'll see a few tricks for arranging icons and using your desktop efficiently.

Cleaning Up Your Desktop

If you're looking at icons on the desktop, the Special menu has a Clean Up Desktop command. (If you're in a window, that command changes to Clean Up Window.) When you select this command, the icons on your desktop will snap onto an invisible grid and line up neatly. Figures 13.1 and 13.2 show a desktop before and after a cleanup.

1. To clean up your desktop, choose Clean Up Desktop from the Special menu. Drag a few icons from your hard disk to the desktop first so that you can see the effects.

2. For an even neater effect, press the Option key while you choose Clean Up Desktop. The command

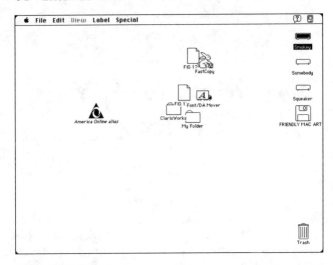

Figure 13.1   A desktop before cleaning up

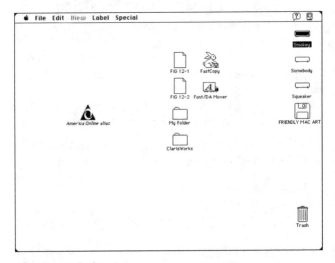

Figure 13.2   The desktop after the cleanup

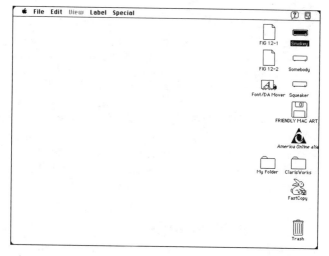

Figure 13.3 Alphabetizing the icons on the desktop

changes to Clean Up All. Look at what happened:
The icons lined up in alphabetical order! Your hard
disk icon and the Trash are always at the top and
bottom, though (Figure 13.3).

Cleaning Up a Window

The Clean Up command changes to Clean Up Window if
you're looking in a window.

1. Double-click on your hard disk icon to open a window. If you're not looking at an icon view in the
   window that appears, first choose by Icon from the
   View menu.
2. Choose Clean up Window from the Special menu,
   to see the effects.

Tip

The Clean Up choice shows the last type of view you used. If you viewed a window by name, for example, the command will be Clean Up by Name.

Cleaning Up a Few Icons

If you don't want all the icons to align on the invisible grid when you choose Clean Up, just select the icons you want to rearrange. Then press Shift before you choose Clean Up, and your selected icons will align neatly.

Making Aliases

One very handy feature of your Macintosh is its ability to make aliases. An **alias** works exactly like the original item but takes up much less space on your disk. You can make aliases of programs and documents you frequently use and keep them on the desktop, where they're easy to find. If you keep aliases on the desktop, you can use them instead of finding the original item buried inside several folders. For example, you might want to keep an alias of your letterhead, created in your word processing program, on the desktop. Anytime you want to write a letter, just double-click on the letterhead alias to start the word processing program and open the document with your return address.

To make an alias, select the item and choose Make Alias from the File menu. An alias icon appears next to the

Figure 13.4   An alias

original item (Figure 13.4). You can drag it into a different folder or put it on the desktop.

Tip

You can put aliases in the Apple menu, too. Just drag the alias to the Apple Menu Items folder in your System Folder (see Lesson 26).

14
Launching Programs and Creating Documents

On your desktop, programs—which are also called **applications**—have fancy icons that represent them. Documents have icons that identify them with the program that created them (Figure 14.1)

- If you double-click on an **application icon**, you'll start ("open" or "launch") that program. Usually, the program will present you with a blank screen where you can start creating a document—drawing in a

Figure 14.1 Application icons and document icons

69

painting program, typing in a word processing program, entering data into a spreadsheet, and so forth.

- If you double-click on a **document icon**, you'll normally start the program that created it and open that particular document.

We'll use TeachText in this and the next lesson, but you can substitute your word processing program if you like. Almost all Macintosh owners have at least one word processing program, and they all work pretty much the same way at the basic level.

Tip

To see which programs you have on your hard disk, double-click on its icon to open it. Then choose by Kind from the View menu. All your applications will be listed at the top.

Creating a New Document

- Locate the TeachText icon (or the icon of your word processing program) and double-click on it to open it (Figure 14.2). You'll see a blank page, where you can just start typing (Figure 14.3).

TeachText

Figure 14.2
The TeachText icon

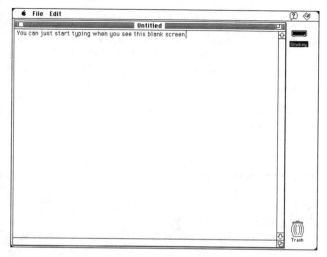

Figure 14.3 The TeachText screen

Tip

A few applications, such as Aldus PageMaker, don't automatically open a blank new document when they start. In such cases, you'll have to choose New from the program's File menu after it starts.

Typing Basics

The **insertion point** is the tiny blinking cursor in the upper left of the screen. When you type, the characters

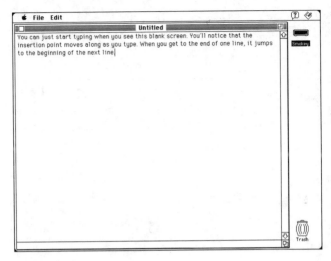

Figure 14.4   Sample text

appear at the insertion point, and the typed text keeps being pushed out in front of them.

- Type a few lines of text, such as the text in Figure 14.4. When you get to the end of a line, don't press the Return key. Instead, watch as the text automatically wraps to the next line. The lines on your screen may not exactly match those in Figure 14.4, but it doesn't matter.

Correcting Mistakes

If you notice that you made a mistake while typing, you can press the Delete key to erase the error and then correct it. Or you can come back to it later and correct it, because after you've typed text, you can click with the mouse to move the insertion point.

Tip
Press the Return key only when you want to end a paragraph or insert a blank line. To delete a blank line, backspace over it with the Delete key.

Selecting Text

To select text, just drag across it. A quick way to select a whole word is to double-click on it. You also can Shift-click to select text: Click once at the beginning of text you want to select, press the Shift key and hold it down, and click at the end of the text. You've used this technique on the desktop to select icons; now you can see how it works to select text.

1. Double-click on the word *line* to select it.
2. Drag across the sentence beginning with *When you get to the end of the line* to select it.
3. Click at the beginning of what you typed, press Shift, and click at the end of what you typed to select it.

Tip
Once text is selected, you can just start typing to replace what's already there without pressing the Delete key first.

Copying, Cutting, and Pasting

Once you've selected text, you can copy it or cut it and then paste it somewhere else.

- Choose Cut from the Edit menu or press ⌘-X to cut the text you've selected. It disappears from the screen. It went to a special part of the Macintosh called the **Clipboard**.

The Clipboard holds the last thing you cut or copied so that you can paste it in another location. Once you select something else and copy or cut it, that selection replaces what's on the Clipboard.

1. To paste the cut text, choose Paste from the Edit menu or press ⌘-V.
2. That selection is still on the Clipboard, even if you've just pasted it. Choose Paste or press ⌘-V again and watch what happens: Another copy of the text appears.

When you copy, the original text stays in place and a copy is made; when you cut, the text you selected disappears.

- Try copying a few words or a sentence: Select some text and press ⌘-C, or choose Copy from the Edit menu. Nothing happens on the screen, but those words are copied to the Clipboard.

Tip

To see what's on the Clipboard, you can choose Show Clipboard from the Edit menu, or you can just press ⌘-V for Paste and see what appears.

- Move the insertion point to the end of the text on your screen and click once. Now press ⌘-V to paste. A copy of the text appears.

Tip

To cancel a selection, just click somewhere outside the highlighted selection.

The Copy, Cut, and Paste commands are on the Edit menu, but you'll use them so often that you might as well get used to their keyboard shortcuts:

⌘-C is the shortcut for Copy.
⌘-X is the shortcut for Cut.
⌘-V is the shortcut for Paste.

15

Saving

The work you do on your computer, such as typing a letter or making a drawing, isn't saved until you use the Save command. If you turn off your Macintosh or if the power goes out before you save, you'll lose whatever work you've done between the last time you saved and the time when the power went out. To save your work, you use the Save command on the File menu of the program you're working in. All programs have a File menu and a Save command.

- To save your document, choose Save from the File menu or press ⌘-S.

Since this is the first time you've saved the document, you're asked to give it a name (Figure 15.1). The name of the folder you're working in is listed at the top of the dialog box (mine is named Sample Documents), and your document will be saved in that folder unless you open a different folder.

If you're not in a folder, you'll see a tiny hard disk icon and the name of your hard disk in the box. If you're at the

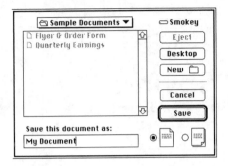

Figure 15.1 Saving a document

desktop, you'll see a tiny blank screen with the word Desktop at the top of the box. You'll see how to move back and forth among these in the next lesson.

1. Type a name for your practice document, such as **My Document**. You can use capital and lowercase letters, and you can have blank spaces between words.

2. Click Save or press the Return key.

Tip

Be sure to give each document a different name. If there's already a document in the folder, which has the same name as the new document you're saving, you'll be asked whether you want to replace it with the document you're saving now. Usually, you *don't* want to do that.

After the first time you save a document, you won't be asked for its name again. You'll see it at the top of the window. All you have to do to save it again is choose Save from the File menu or press ⌘-S. It may seem as though nothing is happening, but if you listen closely, you'll hear your Macintosh as it saves. *Save often so that you won't lose any work if the power goes out.*

The Save As Command

Sometimes, you may want to keep two or more different versions of a document. For example, you may have created a poster for Saturday's garage sale, and you want to change it just a bit so that you can use it again for a bake sale next week. Just give each version of the document a different name by choosing Save As from the File menu, instead of Save.

1. Type another sentence in the document you have on the screen (Figure 15.2).
2. Now, to save this version of My Document—the one with the extra sentence—choose Save As from the File menu. There's no keyboard shortcut for Save As. You'll see the Save As dialog box and My Document will be listed (Figure 15.3).
3. You may want to save the document in a different folder. Click in the box with the tiny folder in it, at the top of the dialog box. You'll see all the folders

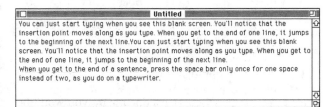

Figure 15.2 Revising the document

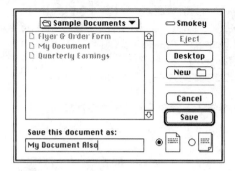

Figure 15.3 Saving the document under another name

leading to the folder you're in (Figure 15.4). To go to a different folder, drag to its name and release the mouse button.

4. Type the name you want this version of the document to have, such as **My Document Also**, and click Save. Be sure to use names that help you remember what your documents really are, not the practice names we're using here.

Saving onto a Floppy Disk

Many times you'll want to save a document onto a floppy disk so that you can give it to someone else or take it to the office or school. You use the Save As command to save a document onto a floppy disk.

1. Locate a floppy disk so that you can practice this skill. If you haven't got one, just read along.
2. Insert the disk in your floppy disk drive.

List of folders leading to where you are

This is the name of your hard disk

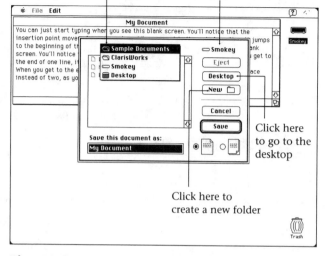

Click here to go to the desktop

Click here to create a new folder

Figure 15.4 Opening a different folder

Tip
If you insert a disk that your Macintosh tells you needs to be initialized, look back at Lesson 7 to understand why.

3. Choose Save As from the File menu. When you see the Save As dialog box, click the Desktop button.

You'll see the floppy disk that's in the drive listed as being on the desktop (Figure 15.5). (Smokey, Somebody, and Squeaker are my three hard disks.) Whatever name it

Floppy disk's name

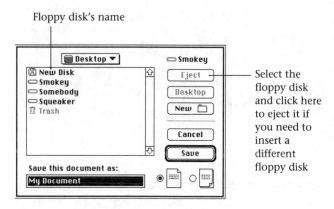

Figure 15.5   A floppy disk that's been inserted in the drive is listed as being on the desktop.

was given when it was initialized appears in the list. Double-click on its name to open it. When its name appears in the Save As dialog box at the top, type a name for your document in the Save this document as: box (Figure 15.6), and it will be saved onto the floppy disk, not onto your hard disk.

> ### *Tip*
> Remember that you also can *copy* a document onto a floppy disk simply by dragging its icon to the floppy disk's icon on the desktop. That way, you have the document on your hard disk and a copy of it on the floppy disk also.

Ready to Quit?

- Close the document's window now. Click in the close box or press ⌘-W.

Figure 15.6 Double-click on the floppy disk's name to make it the open folder in the Save As dialog box.

If you close a document's window before you save it, or if you try to quit without saving a document, you'll be asked if you want to save it. Be sure to save it if you want to keep it and the changes you've made to it! Click Yes to save, No to exit or close without saving, or Cancel to return to the document and stay in the program.

Quitting vs. Closing

There's a difference between **closing a document** and **quitting a program**. When you close a document (by clicking in its close box or pressing ⌘-W), the program itself remains in memory, waiting for you to use it. To work with another document, choose Open from the File menu (for a document you've already created) or New (to start a brand-new document). When you quit (or exit) from a program (by choosing Quit from the File menu or pressing ⌘-Q), you actually shut the program down. To start it again, double-click on its icon.

16

Using the Filing System

There's a difference between creating a **new** document, as you saw in the last lesson, and **open**ing one you've already created, as you'll see in this lesson. If you only closed the document in the preceding lesson, you're still in TeachText or your word processing program. Check the icon on the Applications menu.

- If you want a clean screen where you can create a completely new document, choose New from the File menu.
- If you want to open a document you've already created, choose Open from the File menu.

Opening a Saved Document

- Choose Open from the File menu or press ⌘-O. (If you're looking at a document in TeachText, you'll have to close it before you can open another one.) You'll see the Open dialog box (Figure 16.1). The folder you're in is listed at the top.

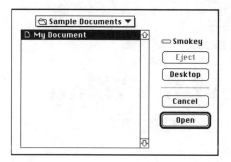

Figure 16.1 The Open dialog box

It looks a lot like the Save As dialog box, doesn't it? Let's practice some more basic skills so that you can understand how to navigate through your system of folders.

Navigating Through Folders

- Click on the box with the tiny folder at the top of the list. Drag down to Desktop and release the mouse button.

Now you're looking at what's on your desktop, including the names of your hard disk and any floppy disks that are in your floppy drives, such as New Disk (Figure 16.2).

1. Double-click on the name of your hard disk and release the mouse button. Now you should see the folders that are on your hard disk (Figure 16.3).
2. Type the first letter of a folder's name to move directly to that part of the alphabet. This is called **speed selecting**. Remember this trick! It's really useful in a long list, because you don't have to scroll.

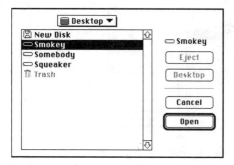

Figure 16.2 The Desktop Contents

3. Double-click on a folder to open it and see the documents that are in it (Figure 16.4).

Tip
The only documents you'll see listed are the ones that the program you're working in can open. Don't be surprised if you don't see something you know is there.

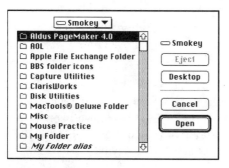

Figure 16.3 Folders on Smokey

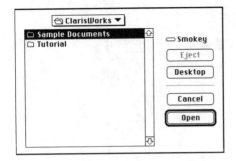

Figure 16.4 Opening another folder

- Click on the tiny folder icon and drag down to the name of your hard disk to see what's on it again.

Tip

If you're looking at what's on your hard disk, you can click on the tiny hard disk icon to see what's on the desktop.

Practice opening folders, looking at what's in them, going to the Desktop, and opening your hard disk, until you get the hang of it. Understanding how your filing system works is important:

- Folders can be nested within folders.
- Your hard disk is at the top level of all folders.
- The desktop is the topmost level, even above your hard disk. It shows other disks, such as floppy disks or any other hard disks you may have (Figure 16.5).

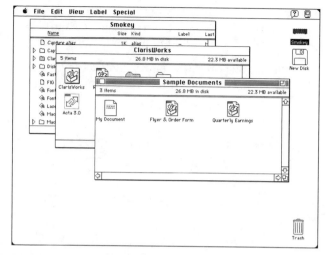

Figure 16.5 Folders within folders on the desktop

Tip

To go to the desktop by using a keyboard shortcut, press ⌘-Shift-up arrow.

• When you find a document you want to open, dou-ble-click on its name.

If you click on the desktop itself while you're practic-ing—the desktop on the screen, not the button or the name that appears in the dialog box—you may activate the Finder instead of your program. Check the Applica-tion menu icon at the far right of the menu bar. It should show the icon of the program you're practicing in. If it shows a tiny Macintosh, you've switched back to the Finder. If this happens, just choose the name of the program you're practicing in from the Application menu.

- When you're through practicing, choose Quit from the File menu to leave TeachText or your word processing program.

Other Ways to Start Programs and Open Documents

In these last two lessons, you've seen the standard ways for opening programs and documents. There are other ways to do this:

- If you double-click on a document's icon, you'll usually open the document and start the program that created it. If the Macintosh can't locate the program that the document belongs to, you'll see a dialog box telling you so.
- You also can drag a document's icon to the icon of the program that created it. When the program's icon turns dark, just release the mouse button, and the program will start, opening the document you dragged.

◆ *Lesson* ◆

17

Switching Between Programs

One of the greatest things about the Macintosh is that you can have several applications in memory and switch between them. You can cut, copy, and paste between different programs, which means that it's easy to put graphics in letters, word processing text in graphics, spreadsheet data in charts—you get the idea. To switch between one program and another, just click in a window of the program you want to switch to.

The secret to knowing which program is active is to watch the icon on the Application menu: It changes to show which program you're really in (Figure 17.1).

Figure 17.1
ClarisWorks is the active program.

Clicking in a window to switch between programs works well if you can see into one of those windows. But sometimes a program's window fills most of the screen. If this is the case, instead of resizing or dragging windows to see what's under them, use the Application menu to switch to a different program or to return to the Finder to start a new program by double-

Figure 17.2　The check mark
indicates which program is active.

clicking on its icon. The Application menu lists all the
programs that are running (Figure 17.2); drag to switch to
a different program.

Sometimes when you're running more than one program, windows cover up other windows that you want to
see into. If you want to see into only the windows of the
active program, select Hide Others from the Application
menu.

 Tip
Press Option while you drag to choose a different
program from the Application menu, and you'll
hide the windows of the other running programs.

You also can hide the windows of the program you're
working in, or choose Show All to see all the windows of
all the programs that are running.

If you don't have a special kind of Macintosh called a
Performa, or if you're not using At Ease, you can skip the
next two lessons.

18

The Performa

Performas are the line of Macintoshes that are sold in stores such as Sears, BizMart, Montgomery Ward, and so forth. A Performa is almost exactly like a Macintosh that you buy in a computer store, except that it uses a special interface to make opening and saving documents even simpler. You won't have to worry about installing system software on it, because it comes already installed. Quite a few programs come installed on a Performa, too.

Although most of the knowledge and skills you use on a regular Macintosh are the same on a Performa, there are only a couple of major differences, and those are in how you start and run programs and where you save documents. The Performa has a special Launcher window for opening programs and a Documents folder for saving documents. This lesson shows you how to use those features. You'll want to take the rest of the lessons in this book, too, to see how to select from menus, rename and select icons, and so forth. See the Epilogue, "Where to Go from Here," for more information about the Performa.

Figure 18.1   The Performa's Launcher window

The Launcher

When you start a Performa, you see a special window called the Launcher (Figure 18.1). The Launcher shows the programs that have been installed on your Performa. Just click once on one of these large, easy-to-hit buttons to start a program.

1. Move the pointer now to Mouse Basics in the Launcher and click once.
2. You'll hear a click, and a tutorial starts that gives you practice in using the mouse to click and drag. To stop the tutorial, press ⌘-. (the clover-leaf shaped key and the period key at the same time). When you're done, come back here.
3. Double-click on the Documents folder on your screen. The Documents folder will open, showing the documents that are already stored on your Performa (Figure 18.2).

To open a document (which automatically starts the program that created it), double-click on a document icon. To open a folder, double-click on its icon.

- Close the Documents folder window by clicking once in the tiny close box at the upper left corner of the screen.

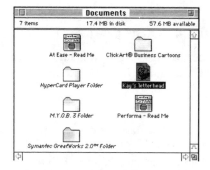

Figure 18.2   The Documents folder window

More About the Launcher

You can move the Launcher window, like any other window on your desktop.

1. Click in the Launcher's title bar (the one with horizontal lines on it at the top) and drag it to a different location; then release the mouse button. It will stay where you put it, even if you turn your computer off and back on again.

> **Tip**
> If the Launcher window gets closed while you practice with your Performa, double-click on the Launcher icon on the desktop to open it again.

2. Try starting a program from the Launcher. Click once on a button. If the Launcher window isn't *active* (only one window at a time can be active),

click twice—once to make the Launcher window active and another time to start the program.

If this is the first time you've used the program you click on, you may be asked to fill out information to personalize your copy.

- Take a few minutes and start the programs you've gotten with your Performa to see what you have. All of them will have different menus, but they'll all have an Apple menu, a File menu, and an Edit menu. Choose Quit from a program's File menu or press ⌘-Q to exit from it. See Lesson 12 for more about choosing from menus.

Saving Documents

The Performa stores all the documents that you save in its Documents folder, which makes them easier for beginners to find. To see how to create a document, go to Lessons 14 and 15 and work through those steps in TeachText.

 Tip
On a Performa, be sure to give each document a different name, because they're all saved in the same Documents folder, and each document has to have a name of its own. If you save two documents with the same name, the second one you save will replace the first one.

Whenever you want to open a document that you've saved, double-click on the Documents folder icon to open it; then double-click on the name of the document.

Running Programs

Although the Performa lets you have more than one program open at once if memory allows (just like any other Macintosh), it's different from a standard Macintosh because it shows you only one program at a time. This makes the Performa easier for beginners to use, because you don't have to figure out which program is active by looking at a clutter of open windows on your Desktop. The programs that are running appear on the Application menu (Figure 18.3).

- To switch to a different program that's already open, choose its name from the Application menu.
- To start a new program running, choose Finder from the Application menu and click on the program's button in the Launcher window.

Making Backups

One of the most important things you can do before you do very much with your Performa is make backups of the documents and programs on its hard disk. You don't get software (except for system software) on floppy disks when you get a Performa, so if something happens to your

Figure 18.3   Choose Finder to get back to the Launcher window.

hard disk, you won't have any copies of the programs unless you do a backup.

The Performa comes with a built-in Backup utility program. Be sure to use it to back up your hard disk just as soon as you can. Click the Apple Backup button in the Launcher window and follow the instructions on the screen. You'll need 20 high-density disks, and the process will take about 45 minutes.

You now have enough information to get you started with your Performa. If you've skipped some of the previous lessons, go back and work through them now.

After You Get Used to Your Performa...

After you've used your Performa awhile, you may want to add programs to the Launcher, delete from it programs you don't use, or get rid of it and the Documents folder altogether.

Customizing the Launcher

As you become more familiar with your Performa, you'll probably want to add new programs that you buy to the Launcher, or delete a program or two from it.

To add a program to the Launcher:

1. Insert the disk that has the program on it into your floppy disk drive. If there's a disk labeled Installer, use it. Then double-click on that disk's icon to open it.

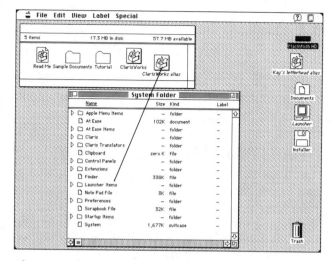

Figure 18.4 Drag an alias to this folder to put it in the Launcher.

2. Double-click on the Installer icon and follow the instructions on the screen.

3. When the program has been installed, locate its icon on your hard disk. You'll probably find it in a folder that has the same name as the program.

4. Select the program icon and choose Make Alias from the File menu. Then drag the alias to the Launcher Items folder in the System Folder (Figure 18.4), and your program will appear in the Launcher.

To delete a program from the Launcher, just drag its icon out of the Launcher Items folder in the System Folder.

Tip
You can put aliases of documents and folders in the Launcher window, too. Make an alias of anything on your hard disk and drag it to the Launcher Items folder, and it will appear in the Launcher. See Lesson 13 for more about aliases.

Bypassing the Documents Folder

After you get accustomed to your Performa, you'll probably decide that you don't want to store every single document you create in that Documents folder. You can store documents in any folder you like. To get rid of the Documents folder, just name it something else and it will stop showing up as the folder that you save into.

Removing the Launcher

To turn your Performa into a Macintosh that works more like a standard Macintosh, you can remove the Launcher.

1. Select Control Panels from the Apple menu.
2. Drag the Launcher icon out of the Control Panels folder. It's not a good idea to store it in your System Folder, but you can store it anywhere else on your hard disk.
3. Open the System Folder. Then open the Startup Items folder and drag the Launcher alias to the Trash. Empty the Trash by choosing Empty Trash from the Special menu.
4. Press Option and click in the close box of one window, and all the windows will close.
5. Restart your Macintosh (select Restart from the Special menu), and you'll no longer see the Launcher.

If you ever want to go back to using the Launcher, locate its icon. Make an alias of it (see Lesson 13) and drag the alias to the Startup Items folder in your System Folder. Put the original Launcher icon back in the Control Panels folder.

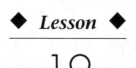

◆ *Lesson* ◆

19

At Ease

At Ease is a program you can purchase from Apple, which makes using a Macintosh (including a Performa) even simpler and easier. When At Ease is installed on your computer, applications are in an Applications folder, Documents are represented by buttons in a Documents folder, and there's no Trash, so nothing can be deleted. Figure 19.1 shows what your startup screen looks like if At Ease is installed.

> **Tip**
>
> If you have small children or if other people have access to your computer, consider getting At Ease. When it's on, no one can delete anything from your hard disk. And you can set it up so that everything that's saved goes onto floppy disks, so no one can change your files, either.

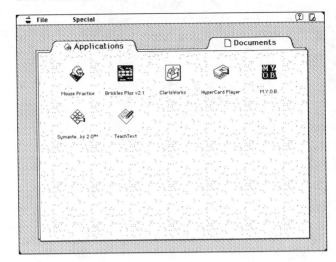

Figure 19.1 The At Ease startup screen

Using At Ease

To start a program in At Ease, click once on its icon in the Applications folder. To open a document, (Figure 19.2), click on the Documents folder tab.

If you don't see a Documents folder, whoever set up At Ease decided that users should save their work onto floppy disks. When you try to save a document, you'll be prompted to insert a floppy disk.

If there are more documents or applications than will fit on one folder, click on the dog-eared tab at the lower right corner of the folder to move from one folder to the next.

If you want to open a document or program that's not in the Documents or Applications folder, choose Open Other from the File menu. You may be asked for a password if At Ease's owner has set one up.

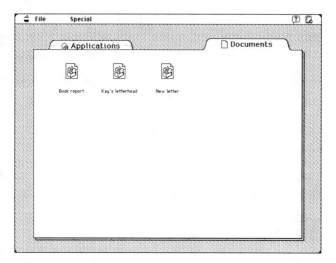

Figure 19.2 The Documents folder

Tip
The animated Mouse Practice tutorial that comes with At Ease is designed for beginning users, especially children.

The At Ease Menus

The menus in At Ease are simpler than those on a regular Macintosh or Performa. For example, there aren't any control panels on the Apple menu, so no one can change the way you've customized your Macintosh. The File menu is much smaller, too, and contains a new command: Go To Finder. You can use this command to switch between At Ease and the standard Macintosh desktop if you know the password the At Ease owner set up. The Special menu allows you only to eject floppy disks, restart your computer, and shut it down. The Application menu icon shows an even smaller Macintosh next to the Finder icon when At Ease is running (Figure 19.3). If you've started more than one program running, you can switch between them by choosing the program you want from the Application menu.

Figure 19.3
The Application menu with At Ease running

 Tip
To get back to At Ease from a program that you're using, choose At Ease from the Application menu. See Lesson 17 for more about using the Application menu.

Turning On At Ease

1. Choose Control Panels from the Apple menu.
2. Double-click on the At Ease Setup icon.
3. Click On.
4. Restart your Macintosh.

Setting Up At Ease

At Ease comes with Mouse Practice set up as the only program in the Applications folder, so you'll want to set it up with the programs you want other people to have access to. You'll also have to decide whether or not they can save their documents onto your hard disk.

Figure 19.4   At Ease Setup

Adding Programs

You can add all or some of the programs on your hard disk
to At Ease's Applications folder.

1. Double-click on the At Ease Setup icon and click
   Select Items (Figure 19.4).
2. Click Gather Applications, then click Add (Figure 19.5).

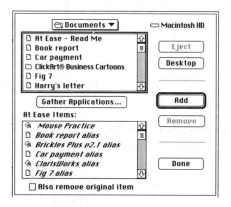

Figure 19.5   Setting up programs

3. At Ease will list all the items it's added at the bottom of the dialog box. You can then go back and select the items you don't want all your users to be able to use. Just click their names and click Remove. Click Done when you've finished.

Saving Documents

You can decide how documents can be saved, too. Double-click on the At Ease icon. Then click Set Up Documents and fill out the dialog box in Figure 19.6.

If you check the Add a button to At Ease box, each time anyone saves a document, a new button will be added to the Documents folder. You probably don't want that. If there's a button for a document or program, your users don't need a password to use it.

> **Tip**
> To have At Ease make a button for an individual item, check the Add to At Ease Items box that appears when you choose Open Other from the File menu.

Figure 19.6 Setting up documents

Click Require a floppy disk if you want people to be able to save their work only onto floppy disks, so that your hard disk doesn't fill up. They'll be asked to insert a floppy disk each time they try to save.

If you keep Add a button to At Ease checked, each time a document is saved, a new button will appear in the At Ease Documents folder.

Setting a Password

For maximum security, set a password so that only users who know the password will be able to get to anything on your hard disk that doesn't have a button in At Ease.

To set a password:

1. Click Set Password in the At Ease Setup box.
2. Fill out the Set Password dialog box (Figure 19.7). Enter a clue about what the password is so that you can remember it! The clue will appear each time At Ease asks for a password.

Figure 19.7 Setting a password

You're in Charge!

With At Ease, you're in charge of who gets to use what. But the day may come when you want to bypass At Ease and go directly to the regular desktop. Instead of starting, turning off At Ease, and restarting, just press the Shift key while your Macintosh is starting, and At Ease won't come up. You'll be asked for the password, though, if you're using one.

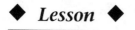

◆ *Lesson* ◆

20

The Desk Accessories

The desk accessories are listed on your Apple menu. They're neat utilities that you can use in any program, because what's on the Apple menu is always available when you're in a program.

Tip

You can put items on your Apple menu, too. See Lesson 26 for details.

The Alarm Clock

Your Macintosh has a built-in clock and calendar, but you'll have to reset the clock twice a year for Daylight Savings time. You can set your system clock with the Alarm Clock desk accessory or with the General Controls panel. The Alarm Clock also lets you set an alarm to remind yourself of an important time.

1. Select Alarm Clock from the Apple menu.
2. Click on the tiny flag icon to open the Alarm Clock (Figure 20.1)

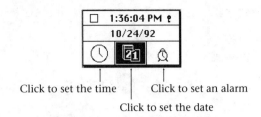

Click to set the time | Click to set an alarm

Click to set the date

Figure 20.1 The open Alarm Clock

3. To change the time, click on the wall clock. Then click on the time that appears in the middle box and use the arrows to change the numbers, or just type the correct numbers for the time.
4. Click on the wall clock again to reset the clock.
5. To set an alarm time, click on the alarm clock. Set the alarm time in the middle panel. Then click on the little keyhole icon on the left so that it turns up.
6. Click the flag icon to close the Alarm Clock to a small window.

When the alarm goes off, you'll hear a beep and the Apple menu icon will flash the Alarm Clock icon. Go to the Alarm Clock on the Apple menu and click on the little keyhole icon to turn it off (down). If you just close the Alarm Clock, it will "ring" again 24 hours later!

Tip

You can paste the date and time anywhere in a document. Open the Alarm Clock, press ⌘-C, go to the document, and press ⌘-V.

Figure 20.2 The Calculator

The Calculator

The Calculator (Figure 20.2) is a built-in 10-key calculator. Click on the numbers to put them in the results box at the top of the Calculator. Click on + for addition, − for subtraction, / for division, and * for multiplication. To get the result of your calculation, click =. To clear the Calculator, click C.

You also can use the keys on the numeric keypad instead of clicking with the mouse.

Tip
You can copy your calculated results into documents. With the result displayed in the active Calculator, press ⌘-C. In your document, press ⌘-V.

The Chooser

You use the Chooser to choose your printer before you can print. Lesson 22 covers this function in more detail.

Key Caps

The Key Caps desk accessory (Figure 20.3) lets you put unusual symbols and accented letters into your documents. Key Caps shows a layout of your keyboard, with the characters that are available in the font you've chosen from the Key Caps menu at the top of the screen.

1. Open the Key Caps desk accessory by choosing it from the Apple menu.
2. Press Shift to see the characters change. Press Option to see other characters. Press Shift and Option together to see if any more characters are available in that font.
3. Choose another font from the Key Caps menu and see what characters are available in it by repeating step 2.
4. Click on a character and watch it appear in the box above the keyboard.

Once you've "typed" a character or word this way, you can drag over the letters or words to select them and then copy and paste them into your documents. Be sure that the font you've selected in the document is the same one you chose in Key Caps!

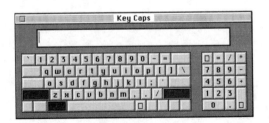

Figure 20.3 Key Caps

Table 20.1 Special Characters

To Create	Symbol Name	Press
•	Bullet	Option-8
…	Ellipsis	Option-;
–	En dash	Option-hyphen
—	Em dash	Option-Shift-hyphen
©	Copyright	Option-g
™	Trademark	Option-2
®	Registration mark	Option-r

You can create some special characters in any font without using Key Caps at all. Table 20.1 shows what they are and how to produce them.

The Note Pad

The Note Pad (Figure 20.4) lets you make short lists of chores to do, names and addresses, and things like that, up to eight pages of notes. To "turn" the pages, click on

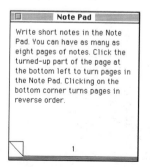

Figure 20.4 The Note Pad

Figure 20.5 The picture Puzzle

the turned-up corner at the lower left of the Note Pad. You can copy your notes and paste them in documents—a great way to keep a few frequently used names and addresses.

The Puzzle

To solve the Puzzles (Figures 20.5 and 20.6), drag the little squares around until you get the complete Apple logo. To switch to a different number Puzzle, choose Clear from the Puzzle's Edit menu.

> **Tip**
>
> To create your own Puzzle, copy a graphic image in your painting or drawing program. Open the Scrapbook and paste. Then open the Puzzle and choose Paste. To get back to the original Puzzle, choose Clear from the Puzzle's Edit menu.

Figure 20.6 The number Puzzle

The Scrapbook

The Scrapbook (Figure 20.7) can store notes, names and addresses, graphic images, and even sounds. Once you've pasted something in the Scrapbook, it stays there, unlike the Clipboard, whose contents are replaced every time you copy or cut. Click on the scroll arrows or use the scroll bar to see what's in your Scrapbook.

To copy text or graphics into the Scrapbook, select what you want to copy in the program you're working in. Open the Scrapbook and paste (⌘-V is the shortcut). To copy something out of the Scrapbook, open the Scrapbook and display the item. Then press ⌘-C to copy it. Go back to your document and paste (⌘-V). To delete an item from the Scrapbook, choose Clear from the Edit menu while the item is displayed.

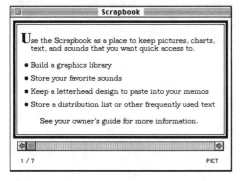

Figure 20.7 The Scrapbook

21

The Control Panels

The control panels let you customize how your Macintosh works. They're on the Apple menu.

- Choose Control Panels from the Apple menu. You'll see the control panels that are on your Macintosh (Figure 21.1)

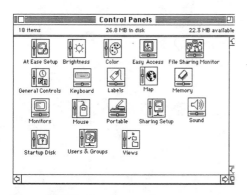

Figure 21.1 The Control Panels

119

These are some of the control panels that come with your Macintosh. Different models of Macs, such as the PowerBook, have extra control panels. You can acquire more by buying them or getting them as freeware. We'll take a quick look at what they do, and you can explore them on your own. The ones you'll use most often are General Controls, Mouse, Keyboard, and Sound.

General Controls

The General Controls panel (Figure 21.2) lets you change the desktop pattern and color. It also lets you set the rate at which the menus and the insertion point blink, as well as change the date, time, and the time format.

To see the General Controls panel or any of the other control panels, double-click on its icon. Close it by clicking in its close box or pressing ⌘-W when you're through.

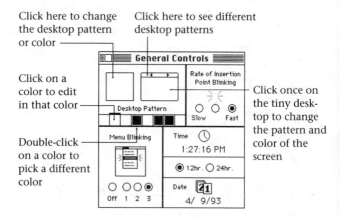

Figure 21.2   The General Controls panel

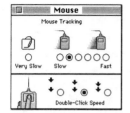

Figure 21.3 The Mouse control panel

Mouse

The Mouse control panel (Figure 21.3) lets you adjust how the mouse works. If you set Mouse Tracking to Fast, the pointer on the screen will move twice as fast as the mouse on your real desktop.

Click a different Double-Click Speed button and watch the finger give a demonstration of that double-click.

Keyboard

The Keyboard control panel (Figure 21.4) lets you change how fast a key repeats when you hold it down. If you set Delay Until Repeat to Off, keys *won't* repeat at all.

Sound

The Sound control panel (Figure 21.5) lets you pick a sound to use as your Macintosh's beep. If your Macintosh has a built-in microphone, the Sound control panel also lets you record sounds.

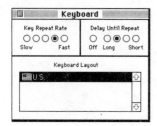

Figure 21.4   The Keyboard control panel

If you have a microphone, here's how to record your
own sound.

1. Plug the microphone into the microphone plug on
   the back of the computer.
2. Open the Sound control panel and click Add. You'll
   see the dialog box in Figure 21.6.
3. Click Record and speak into the microphone.

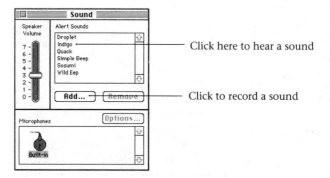

Figure 21.5   The Sound control panel

Figure 21.6   Recording a sound

4. When you've finished recording, click Stop.
5. Click Play to hear your sound.
6. To save your sound, click Save and give your sound a name. It will appear in the list of alert sounds in the Sound control panel.

Other Common Control Panels

There are a few other control panels you may use from time to time: Color, Map, Views, and Labels.

Color

The Color control panel (Figure 21.7) lets you change colors for window borders and text that's highlighted.

Click here to
see more colors

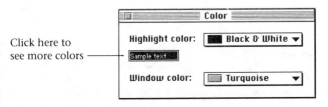

Figure 21.7   The Color control panel

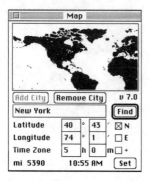

Figure 21.8   The Map control panel

Map

The Map control panel (Figure 21.8) lets you see the local time all over the world, as well as the distances between cities. Press the Option key and click Find to see the cities that are stored in the Map. To add a city, click on its location, enter its name, and click Add.

> **Tip**
> Paste the color Map from the Scrapbook into this control panel to get a nicer map.

Views

The Views control panel (Figure 21.9) lets you pick a different font and size for Finder windows and lets you choose how you want icons to be aligned on the screen, among other things.

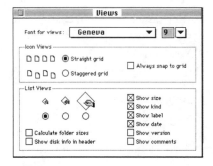

Figure 21.9 The Views control panel

Labels

You use the Labels control panel (Figure 21.10) to set up the system of colors and labels you want to use on the Labels menu.

Special Control Panels

The rest of the control panels are pretty specialized, and you'll normally use them only from time to time. You may never use some of them at all.

Figure 21.10 The Labels control panel

- The Monitors control panel lets you change the number of colors your monitor displays, or switch to black-and-white if you want to.

- Easy Access lets you use the keys on the numeric keypad instead of the mouse. It's designed for people who have trouble using a mouse.

- The Brightness control panel lets you adjust the brightness of your screen. It works only on Macintoshes that don't have a brightness knob on the monitor.

- The Memory control panel lets you change memory settings. The options you'll see depend on the particular model of Macintosh you have.

- The Startup Disk control panel is used only if you have more than one hard disk. It lets you choose which disk to start from.

Networking Control Panels

The rest of the control panels are concerned with setting up your Macintosh for networking. If you have two Macintoshes, you can easily connect them and have your own network, but we won't cover networking in this book. These control panels are called Sharing Setup, Users & Groups, File Sharing Monitor, and Network.

- The Sharing Setup control panel lets you identify your computer on a network and set your password.

- The Users & Groups control panel lets you decide who can have access to files on your Macintosh.

- The File Sharing Monitor control panel lets you see which items you're sharing on a network and who else is using them.
- The Network control panel lets you choose which network to connect to. It won't appear if you aren't on a network.

◆ *Lesson* ◆

22
Printing

Before you can print, you'll have to connect your printer to your Macintosh and switch it on.

1. Once you've done that, select Chooser from the Apple menu.

All the icons for Apple printers should appear in the Chooser, because they're installed along with the system software. If you have a non-Apple printer, you may need to read the instructions that came with it to get its icon to appear in the Chooser.

2. In the Chooser, click on the icon representing your printer (Figure 22.1).

3. Click on the icon that represents which port the printer's connected to. Most of the time, your printer will be on the printer port—the one that looks like a tiny printer.

4. Click the Inactive button if you're not on a network.

5. Click On next to Background Printing if you have a laser printer and you want to be able to keep on working while your documents are being printed.

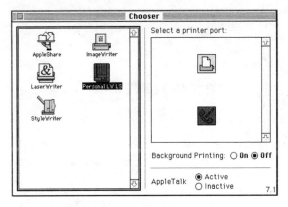

Figure 22.1   Choosing a printer

Tip
If you have a laser printer and you *don't* see the Background Printing button, make sure the Print-Monitor icon as well as the LaserWriter icon are in your System Folder. (See Lesson 26.)

Setting Print Options

- Choose Page Setup from the File menu to select the print options you want (Figure 22.2). The Page Setup dialog box is different for each type of printer.

Tip
If the Page Setup command is dimmed, click on a document icon in the Finder.

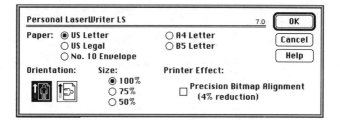

Figure 22.2 A Page Setup dialog box for a Personal LaserWriter

Here are a few of the things you may see:

- Orientation refers to how the image is printed on the page.
- Paper sizes given are the most popular paper sizes. US Letter is 8.5 by 11 inches; US Legal is 8.5 by 14 inches; a No. 10 Envelope is a standard business-size envelope; A4 is a popular size in Europe; and B5 is a popular size in Japan.
- If you want the page reduced, you may be able to choose a reduction percentage under Size. With certain printers, you also may see a Scale choice and a percentage.
- Check Precision Bitmap Alignment if you're printing bitmapped graphics (those that are created in a painting program).
- You may be able to choose a print quality if you're using an ImageWriter (laser printers print in one quality only—high). If you choose Draft, you won't get any graphics in your printed document, and a hard-to-read font will be used. But Draft printing is fast.

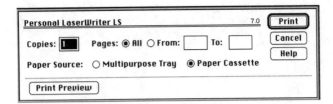

Figure 22.3   A Print dialog box

- On an ImageWriter, you may see a Tall Adjusted button. Click it if you don't want circles to come out as ovals.

Printing

Printing on a Macintosh is very easy—all you do is choose Print from the File menu or use the shortcut ⌘-P to print the document you're viewing on the screen. You'll see a dialog box asking various things, depending on which printer you have and which program you're using (Figure 22.3).

Tip
To print just one page, such as page 3, enter 3 in both the From and To boxes.

Switching Printers

If you have more than one printer, you switch from one to the other by clicking on its icon in the Chooser. After you change from one printer to another, you'll see a message warning you to use the Page Setup command in all the programs you have running. You don't need to change anything; just open the Page Setup dialog box so that your program will know you've switched printers. Documents have to be formatted in a slightly different way for each kind of printer.

Printing in the Finder

Usually, you'll print by using a program's Print command when you have the document you want to print displayed on the screen. You also can print from the Finder by highlighting the icons of the documents you want to print and then choosing Print. The Macintosh launches the program or programs that were used to create the documents, and shows you a Print dialog box for each document.

Printing a Window

A Print Window command on the File menu lets you print the contents of the window that's currently active. If no window is active, that command changes to Print Desktop. Either of these commands is useful for printing out a listing of all the files on a disk.

Suppressing a LaserWriter's Startup Page

If you have a laser printer, you can conserve paper by turning off the option that prints a startup page every time you switch on the LaserWriter. Find the LaserWriter Font Utility. If you can't find it on your hard disk, it's on the Tidbits disk that came with your Macintosh, and you can copy it onto your hard disk.

Choose Start Page Options from its Utilities menu, click the Off button, and choose Quit from the File menu (or press ⌘-Q) to exit from the LaserWriter Font Utility.

Tip
While you're in the LaserWriter Font Utility, you can give your printer a name by choosing Name Printer from the Utilities menu.

PrintMonitor

PrintMonitor is a utility that takes over when you're using a laser printer with background printing turned on in the Chooser. It lets you check how far along your printing jobs are, cancel printing documents that are in line to print, or set a time for printing to start. PrintMonitor also will tell you when it's time to reload the paper tray.

To go to PrintMonitor, choose its name from the Application menu (Figure 22.4). You'll see the PrintMonitor window (Figure 22.5).

You can change the printing order by dragging a document's name to a different position in the lineup. To cancel printing a document, click on its name and then

Figure 22.4   To get to PrintMonitor, choose it from the Application menu.

The name of the
document that's being
printed now   The name of the printer

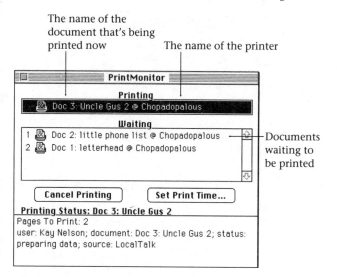

Figure 22.5 The PrintMonitor window

click the Remove button that will appear. To cancel the
document that's being printed, click the Cancel Printing.

PrintMonitor resides in the Extensions folder inside
your System Folder. To set preferences about how you
want it to work, double-click on its icon there and choose
Preferences from its File menu.

Tip

To cancel all printing jobs, close the PrintMonitor
window by clicking in its close box.

Choosing Stop from the File menu just suspends
printing.

Problems with Printing?

Here are some of the most common sources of printing problems, and how to solve them:

- Make sure the printer's power is turned on, that it has paper, and that the paper tray (if it has one) is all the way in.
- Check to see that all the cable connections are tight.
- Go to the Chooser on the Apple menu and make sure you've selected the icon of the printer you're using.
- If you're printing on an ImageWriter, make sure its Select light is on.
- Make sure your hard disk isn't completely full. The printing process requires a little hard disk space. You may need to delete a few outdated files to make room.

 Tip
To see how much space you have left on a disk, use the Views control panel and check the Show disk info in the header box.

- As a last resort, turn off the printer, wait a minute, and try printing again. This often helps for no apparent reason; it's like peering under the hood of your car.

If you're printing a document that has a lot of graphics or fonts in it, be prepared for slow printing.

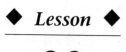

◆ *Lesson* ◆

23

Fonts

One of the greatest things about your Macintosh is that you have quite a selection of fonts to choose from, so you can get different effects in the documents you create. **Fonts** are also called **typefaces**, and they're collections of letters and symbols.

Tip

For a professional, polished look, try not to use more than two or three different fonts in the same document.

Installing New Fonts

Adding new fonts to your collection is easy. Here's how to install a new font onto your Macintosh:

1. Exit from any programs you're running.
2. Put the disk with the new fonts on it in your floppy drive; then double-click on its icon.
3. Fonts usually come in **font suitcases**: Double-click on a font suitcase to open it (Figure 23.1).

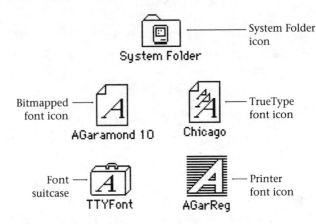

Figure 23.1   Font icons

4. Drag the icons of the fonts you want to the icon of your System Folder. Shift-click to select just a few fonts, or to install all the fonts in the suitcase, just drag the suitcase to the System Folder icon.

You can see a sample of what a font looks like before you install it. Just double-click on its icon (Figure 23.2).

Jagged Edges?

If you're printing characters that have jagged edges or look weird, you're probably using a bitmapped font in a size that it doesn't come in. If this happens to you, select a size represented by outlined numbers on your Font or Character menu (Figure 23.3) for better results.

Figure 23.2 Font samples

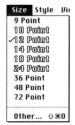

Figure 23.3 Choose an outlined size if you get jagged printing.

♦ *Lesson* ♦

24
Finding Things

Instead of hunting through folders one by one, you can use the Find command on the File menu to have your Macintosh locate the file you're looking for. It's much faster than clicking on folders to find things.

Simple Finding

1. Go to the desktop if you're not already there. Click on any part of the desktop that you can see.
2. Suppose that you want to find the folder you created named My Other Folder. Choose Find from the File menu, then type **my other folder** in the Find box (Figure 24.1). You can use all lowercase letters; capital letters don't matter.

Tip

You don't have to know the whole name of what you're looking for. If you know only a word or two of its name, just type that in the Find box.

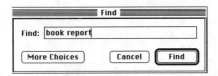

Figure 24.1 Finding a file

3. Click the Find button or press Return. The Macintosh will find a file whose name matches what you type and show you where it is, with its name highlighted so that you can just double-click on it to open it. If the Macintosh can't find anything that matches, you'll hear a beep.

4. If that particular file isn't the one you're looking for, choose Find Again from the File menu, or use the shortcut ⌘-G (think of it as aGain). Keep on going until you find the file you want.

Remember, a "file" can be a document, a folder, a control panel or desk accessory, or a program, so you can look for just about anything.

More Complex Finding

To do more complicated finding, click the More Choices button in the Find dialog box.

1. Choose Find from the File menu or press ⌘-F. Click More Choices, and you'll see another dialog box (Figure 24.2).

2. Say that you want to locate all the files, all at once instead of one at a time, that have *Folder* in their names. Type **folder**, check the all at once box, and then click Find.

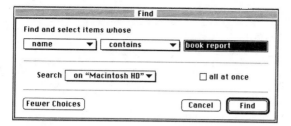

Figure 24.2 More choices

The Macintosh will find everything whose name contains *folder*. You'll see a little thermometer bar indicating that it's searching and how many items it has found. Then it will open a window onto your hard disk and highlight the items it has found. Even if they're buried several folders deep, it will expand the folders they're in. As you scroll through the window, you'll see the highlighted items that match.

If any of the items it finds aren't on your hard disk— maybe they're in the Trash or out on the desktop—you'll see a message telling you to use Find Again to see these items.

Tip
To go back to the simple Find dialog box, click Fewer Choices.

Many Choices
Many different kinds of choices lie within this dialog box. Click on any of the arrows to see a list of what you can

Figure 24.3 More items you can choose

choose. Figure 24.3 shows the choices you can make if you click on *name*.

You also can tell the Macintosh *where* you want it to search. Normally it will search your hard disk, but you can tell it to search any floppy disks you've inserted, search the desktop, search just the active window, or search items that have been selected. To do this, choose what you want to search from the pop-up list next to Search.

Complicated Searches

Suppose you want to find all the files that have Carmen in their names and that were created after August 20, 1993. First, search for all the files whose names contain Carmen. Then, without clicking anywhere, do another search. (If you click anywhere, you'll deselect all the files the Macintosh has found!) This time, search "the selected items" whose "date created" "is after" August 20, 1993. Today's date will appear; to change it to a different date, click on it and then click on the little arrows next to it (Figure 24.4).

Now when you click Find, you'll locate only the files that have the word *Carmen* in their names and that were created after August 20.

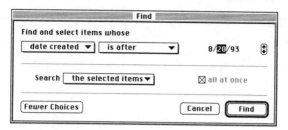

Figure 24.4 Searches within searches

Tip
Find files by creation date from time to time, to see which files on your disk are way out of date. Maybe you can delete a few.

◆ *Lesson* ◆

25

Shortcuts

You've seen keyboard shortcuts mentioned often as we've worked through these lessons. Using keyboard shortcuts can save you a lot of time. After you've become accustomed to your Macintosh, you'll probably want to use them a lot.

There also are other shortcuts that combine using the keyboard and the mouse, and these are really valuable, too. You've seen many of these in the previous lessons; here they are all together.

Menu Shortcuts

Table 25.1 lists some of the most often used menu shortcuts. Rest assured that there are a lot more of them; these are just the common ones that appear in the menus of almost all programs.

To use a ⌘ key shortcut, press the Command key ⌘ and type the appropriate letter key at the same time.

In the manuals that come with your programs, you may see keyboard shortcuts listed in all sorts of different ways,

147

Table 25.1 Menu Keyboard Shortcuts

Shortcut	Command
⌘-C	Copy
⌘-X	Cut
⌘-V	Paste
⌘-N	New document (or folder)
⌘-O	Open
⌘-W	Close window
⌘-S	Save
⌘-Q	Quit

such as ⌘+S or ⌘-S or ⌘ S. They all mean the same thing: Press both those keys at once. Sometimes you'll need to press three keys at once, such as ⌘-Shift-D.

Other Shortcuts

Table 25.2 lists shortcuts you can use in dialog boxes.

Table 25.2 Dialog Box Shortcuts

Shortcut	Result
Press Return	Clicks the button with the heavy border around it
Press ⌘-. (Command and the period key)	Closes a dialog box without making any changes and usually cancels an operation
Press Esc	Closes a dialog box without making any changes

Table 25.3 Desktop Keyboard Shortcuts

Shortcut	Result
⌘-E	Ejects the disk in the floppy drive.
⌘-Y	Puts a file back where it came from. (It also ejects a floppy disk if you've selected the disk's icon.)

Desktop Shortcuts

When you're working at the desktop, other shortcuts are available, as shown in Table 25.3.

Shortcuts that combine the mouse and keys are available, too, as detailed in Table 25.4.

To see even more shortcuts that work at the desktop, choose Finder Shortcuts from the Help menu (Figure 25.1).

Mouse Shortcuts

Table 25.5 lists common and useful mouse shortcuts that you'll use all the time.

Now you're a power user! But check out the last two lessons for some important information.

Table 25.4 Mouse-Keyboard Shortcuts

Shortcut	Result
Press Option and click in *one* close box	Closes all the open windows.
Press Option and drag an icon	Copies the icon into another folder instead of moving it.
Press Option and choose Clean Up from the Special menu	Aligns and sorts icons.
Press ⌘ and click on a window's name	Displays the folders you're in. (This shortcut works only on windows you're looking at on the desktop.)
Press Shift and click on icons	Selects more than one icon at once.
Press the Option key and keep it down as you open folders	The folders that are already open close as you open new ones.
Press the ⌘ key and click on the title of the window	Displays the list of folders leading to where you are.

Figure 25.1 The first screen of Finder shortcuts

Table 25.5 Mouse Shortcuts

Shortcut	Result
Drag a disk icon to the Trash	Ejects the disk.
Double-click on an icon	Opens the icon.
Double-click on a word	Selects the word.
Click outside an icon and drag	Selects the icons that are next to that icon.

◆ *Lesson* ◆

26

Important Information

Most of the time, you'll never even think about what your Macintosh is doing behind the scenes. There are a few things you should know about how it works, though. The most basic things you should know are the differences between the two kinds of memory and how your system software is organized.

Memory vs. Storage

There are two kinds of memory: **RAM**, or random access memory, and **storage**. Both of them are measured in bytes, kilobytes (K), or megabytes (Mb), so it's easy to confuse them. You may have 20 megabytes of space left on your hard disk and still run out of memory, because you're running out of the *other kind* of memory—RAM.

Tip
Think of a byte as one character. A kilobyte is roughly a thousand characters. A megabyte is roughly a thousand kilobytes.

Random access memory is the memory that's used to store the programs and documents you're working on *while you're working on them.* **Storage memory (disk space)** is where they're stored permanently. When you save, you're putting what you worked on in storage, just as though you've taken a document and put it into a file drawer. What's in RAM (your work) isn't saved when you turn off your computer or lose power—unless you've saved it.

- Most Macintoshes nowadays have at least 2Mb of RAM. The more RAM, the more programs you can run and the more documents you can have open at the same time. To add RAM, you buy it as chips that you install (or have someone else install) inside your computer.

- How much hard disk space you have depends on which model of Macintosh you have, but you'll probably have at least 40Mb. To add hard disk space, you can buy another hard disk and plug it into the back of your Mac.

Your System Software

Your system software is stored in a folder named System Folder on your hard disk. Inside the System Folder are several other folders and icons—even more than those shown in Figure 26.1. Normally, you don't need to be concerned about what these are or what they do, but if you ever need to know, this information can be important.

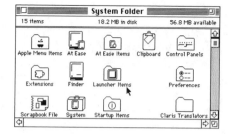

Figure 26.1   The contents of a System Folder

Tip

Don't rename this folder! It needs to be called
System Folder. Keep the System file and Finder in
that System Folder, or you might not be able to
start your Macintosh. In fact, keep all the folders
that you find in your System Folder there. Don't
move them.

The System File

The System file contains the instructions that operate
your Macintosh. You can double-click on the System file
to see some of what's in it. It also contains sounds and
fonts (in Systems 6 and 7.0). In System 7.1, fonts are
stored in a separate Fonts folder. Double-click on a font
icon to see a sample of the font. Double-click on a sound
icon to hear the sound.

The Finder

In your System Folder, the Finder file keeps track of what's on the desktop and where you've stored files. You can't open it to see what's in it.

The Clipboard, Scrapbook, and Note Pad Files

The Clipboard, Scrapbook, and Note Pad files are also stored in your System Folder. You can open these to see what's in them.

Tip
To keep separate Scrapbooks, rename the Scrapbook file so that you can make a new Scrapbook. To get the original Scrapbook back, name it Scrapbook file again.

The Apple Menu Items Folder

The Apple Menu Items Folder holds the icons for the items that are listed on your Apple menu. All you have to do to put an item on the Apple menu is drag its icon to your Apple Menu Items folder. You can put documents, programs, your letterhead—whatever you use most often—on your Apple menu.

Tip
Put aliases (see Lesson 13) in your Apple Menu Items folder and keep the originals where they belong.

The Control Panels Folder

The Control Panels folder holds all the control panels that come with your Macintosh. There are lots of other handy control panels available for purchase or free from user groups or electronic bulletin boards (see "Where to Go from Here" in the Epilogue), such as SoundMaster, which plays a sound when you shut down, restart, or insert a disk. When you get a new control panel, drag it to your closed System Folder. The Mac will place it correctly in your Control Panels folder.

Tip

You can open a control panel by double-clicking on it in the System Folder, as well as by choosing Control Panels from the Apple menu.

The Extensions Folder

The Extensions folder holds files and utilities that extend your Macintosh's capabilities, such as printer icons or PrintMonitor. It also holds programs that change your cursor, display a clock, and so forth. You'll see these kinds of files referred to as "startup documents" or "extensions." It's fun to acquire lots of these (see "Where to Go from Here" in the Epilogue); to install them, just drag them to your closed System Folder.

Because these files go into action when you start up your Macintosh, they can sometimes conflict with one another and your computer may start acting weird. To disable all your extensions, hold down the Shift key when you start your Macintosh.

Tip
To install a new font, sound for your system beep, control panel, or extension, just drag it to the *closed* System Folder. The Macintosh will figure out which folder it's supposed to go in.

The Preferences Folder

The Preferences folder has files that store settings about how you want your programs and the Finder to work. You can't open anything in this folder, and your programs take care of putting items in it, so don't worry about it.

Tip
If you forget your At Ease password, start your Macintosh with the Utilities or Disk Tools disk in the floppy drive. Then open the System Folder and drag the At Ease Preferences icon to the Trash. Restart. Now you can use the At Ease Setup control panel to set a new password. Don't tell anybody.

The Startup Items Folder

If there's a document or program that you want to open automatically each time you start your Macintosh, drag its icon (or an alias of it) to the Startup Items folder.

Tip
To play a startup sound, drag the sound's icon (not an alias) to your Startup Items folder. If your Mac has a built-in microphone, you can have lots of fun with this!

Macintosh Models

A wide variety of Macintoshes are available. Table 26.1 lists the models on the market as this book went to the printer. Your Macintosh may be listed there as "discontinued," but this means only that Apple isn't marketing it any more. You can still get service on it from an Apple dealer, and you can usually upgrade it to a newer version.

All these models have an internal hard disk for storage and at least one floppy disk drive. The simplest way to add more storage capacity is to purchase an external hard disk and just plug it into the back of your Mac. Most Macintoshes (see Table 26.1) have a high-density disk drive called a SuperDrive or FDHD drive (for "floppy disk, high density"). If you have a SuperDrive, you can use high-

Table 26.1 Macintosh Models

Model	Maximum RAM	Super-Drive	Notes
Plus	4Mb	No	Discontinued
SE	4Mb	Yes	Discontinued
SE/30	128Mb	Yes	Discontinued
Classic	4Mb	Yes	Discontinued
Classic II Performa 200	10Mb	Yes	Available
Color Classic	10Mb	Yes	Available
LC	10Mb	Yes	Discontinued
LC II Performa 400, 405, 430	10Mb	Yes	Available

(continued)

Table 26.1 *(continued)*

Model	Maximum RAM	Super-Drive	Notes
LC III Performa 450	36Mb	Yes	Available
II	68Mb	Yes	Discontinued
IIx	128Mb	Yes	Discontinued
IIcx	128Mb	Yes	Discontinued
IIci	128Mb	Yes	Discontinued
IIsi	65Mb	Yes	Discontinued
II vx Performa 600	68Mb	Yes	Available
Centris 610	68Mb	Yes	Available
Centris 650	136Mb	Yes	Available
IIfx	128 Mb	Yes	Discontinued
Quadra 700	64Mb	Yes	Discontinued
Quadra 900	256Mb	Yes	Discontinued
Quadra 950	256Mb	Yes	Available
Quadra 800	136Mb	Yes	Available
PowerBook 100/140/145	8Mb	Yes	Discontinued
PowerBook 160	14Mb	Yes	Available
PowerBook 170	8Mb	Yes	Discontinued
PowerBook 180	16Mb	Yes	Available
Duo 210/320	24Mb	Yes	Available

density disks (see Lesson 7); if not, you're restricted to using 800K (double-density) disks.

No matter which model you have, it can be upgraded in some way, even if it's only to add more RAM (random-access memory). You need at least 4Mb to run System 7 effectively, and 8Mb should be your minimum if you use large application programs like Microsoft Excel or Word 5.1. Adding RAM is relatively inexpensive, and your dealer can do it for you.

◆ *Lesson* ◆

27

Getting Out of Trouble

Sometimes, things may not work quite as you might expect. Fortunately, the Macintosh gives you visual clues or messages about what the problem usually is.

Can't Save or Copy?

If you get the message that a floppy disk is full, that there's not enough room to copy files onto a disk, or that the disk is locked, you won't be able to save or copy anything on it. To solve this problem, you can either:

- Eject the disk, put a different floppy disk in the drive and try saving or copying again.
- Delete something from the floppy disk, empty the Trash, and then save or copy.
- If the message says that the disk is locked, take the disk out of the drive and close the write-protect hole.

Can't Open a Document?

Sometimes when you double-click on a document, the Macintosh will tell you that it can't open it because it can't find the program that originally created the document.

- Try locating the program you used to create the document. You may have a copy of it on a floppy disk.
- Try starting a similar program and then use its Open command to open the document. For example, most word processing programs can open documents created by other word processing programs.

Out of Memory?

If you get a message that you're running out of memory and you need to increase the "application's memory size," that's what you must do.

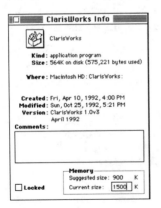

Figure 27.1   A Get Info box

- Highlight the program's icon. Then choose Get Info from the File menu. In the Get Info box (Figure 27.1), enter a larger memory size.

Sad Mac?

The Sad Mac icon (Figure 27.2) indicates problems with your system software. You may need to install your system software again.

If you need to install system software again, locate the disks that came with your Macintosh. Put the Installer disk in the floppy drive and turn on the power. Then follow the instructions on the screen.

Figure 27.2
Sad Mac icon

Tip

If you've added a lot of fonts, sounds, desk accessories, and so forth to your Macintosh, drag them out of the System Folder on your hard disk before you install new system software. That way, you can just drag them back to the System Folder when you're through installing, and you won't have to look for the original disks those items came on to reinstall them.

Question Mark?

If you see a question mark icon (Figure 27.3) when you start your Mac, your hard disk isn't being recognized as a startup disk.

- Find the Disk Utilities or Disk Tools disk that came with your system software. Turn the power to your computer off and put that disk in the floppy drive. Turn the power back on, and your Macintosh should start.

Figure 27.3
Question Mark icon

- You're not through yet, though. You need to repair your hard disk. See Disk First Aid below.

An X Icon?

This icon (Figure 27.4) also indicates a damaged startup disk or a disk that doesn't have any system software on it.

Figure 27.4
X icon

- Try starting with a different startup disk in your floppy drive, such as Install 1 or the Disk Tools or Utilities disk.
- Then use Disk First Aid to repair the damaged disk.

Disk First Aid

The Disk First Aid utility (Figure 27.5) that comes with your Macintosh often can repair a disk. To use it:

Disk First Aid

Figure 27.5
Disk First Aid

1. Put the Utilities or Disk Tools disk (they have different names, depending on

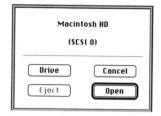

Figure 27.6 Choosing the disk
to be repaired

which version of the system software you're using)
in the floppy drive.
2. Double-click on the disk icon; then double-click on
the Disk First Aid icon.
3. In Disk First Aid (Figure 27.6), click the Drive button
until you see the name of the disk you want to
repair.
4. Click Open and then choose Repair Automatically
from the Options menu that you'll see.
5. Click the Start button to start the process.

If the disk can be repaired, Disk First Aid will report that
the repair is completed, or that no repair was necessary.

Routine Maintenance

Just like you change the oil in your car, you need to do a
little preventive maintenance on your Macintosh. Do this
by "rebuilding the desktop" about once a month: Hold
down the ⌘ and Option keys while you start up. You'll be
asked if you want to rebuild the desktop, so click OK.

Epilogue
Where to Go from Here

If you're interested in finding out more about your Macintosh, try some of the resources—books, user groups, information utilities, magazines—listed here.

Books

The Little System 7.1 Book ($12, Peachpit Press, 800/283-9444)
by Kay Yarborough Nelson

This small book explains how to use even the most sophisticated features of System 7.0 and 7.1 in clear, easy-to-read language.

Voodoo Mac ($21.95, Ventana Press, 919/942-0220)
by Kay Yarborough Nelson

You don't have to be very advanced to do great things with your Macintosh. If you're interested in tricks and shortcuts on your Macintosh, this is a great collection of them.

The Performa: A Visual QuickStart ($12, Peachpit Press, 800/283-9444)
by Kay Yarborough Nelson

If you're absolutely a beginner with a Performa, this profusely illustrated book will show you, screen by screen, how to use it.

User Groups

User groups are a good way to get help and information about using your Macintosh. Use these phone numbers, or call Apple at 800/538-9696 to get a phone number of a user group near you.

East Coast

The Boston Computer Society/Macintosh (BCS/MAC)
617/864-0712

New York MacUsers' Group
212/473-1600

Washington, D.C.

Washington Apple Pi
301/654-8060

West Coast

Berkeley Macintosh Users' Group
BMUG
510/549-BMUG

Los Angeles

Los Angeles Macintosh User Group (LAMG)
310/278-5264

USC Mac User Group
213/278-5264

Seattle

MacAnt
206/441-5352

In Between

Call Apple's User Group Information number, 800/538-9696, for the group nearest you.

Information Utilities

If you have a modem, you can connect to many electronic bulletin boards and information utilities. Most user groups have electronic bulletin boards, too. If you've never used one before, try America Online; it's easiest, and it works just like your Macintosh. All of these come with free time that you can use while you learn. America Online gives you the most free time—five hours.

America Online
18619 Westwood Center Drive
Vienna, VA 22182
800/227-6365

CompuServe
5000 Arlington Centre Blvd.
PO Box 20212
Columbus, OH 43220
800/848-8990

GEnie
401 N. Washington St.
Rockville, MD 20850
800/638-9636

Magazines

Macworld
Subscription number: 800/234-1038

MacUser
Subscription number: 800/627-2247

Index